the new jewelry
trends+traditions

PETER DORMER AND RALPH TURNER

the new jewelry
trends+traditions

REVISED EDITION

with 262 illustrations, 129 in color

THAMES AND HUDSON

Captions to photographs: where one figure only is given this refers to the object's greatest dimension.

Illustration Acknowledgments

Abel, Hans Jørgen 212; Bachhofer, Joss 22, 23, 191; Basen, Rien 13, 207 (Stedelijk Museum, Amsterdam); Beddington, Rose p.177; Carpenter, Ray p.12; Cleveland Contemporary Jewelry Collection, Middlesbrough 214; Contemporary Art Society, London 220; Cripps, David p.13, 11, 12, 48–9, 60, 64–5, 72, 80, 82, 96–7, 102, 111, 113, 121, 123–4, 126–9, 133, 152, 160, 163, 169, 202; Degen, Joël 20–1, 50–1, 83, 106–8, 112, 157, 221, 222; Gollings, Kate 209; Griebsch, John p.19 (Barry Merritt); Haartsen, Tom 14, 15, 90, 114; Hanson, Bob 74; Helen Drutt Gallery p.27, p.116, 19, 29–32, 36, 98–9, 127, 130–1, 134, 139–41, 156; Hill, Tim 66–8; Hinrichs, Dieter 25; Hogers/Versluys 135, 173, 198; Internationale Schmuckszene, Handwerksmesse 210; Kukulies, Achim p.181 (right); Kung, Johsel Nam 136, 138, 158; Künzli, Otto p.25, 8, 28, 47, 59, 68–9, 144–7, 150, 164–8, 173, 204; Lüttge, Thomas 144, 154; Massey, Andrew 217; Nieman, Julian p.12 (Gerda Flöckinger); Powell, Dean 227, 228 (Aaron Faber Galley, New York); Ramsdale, Jack 215 (Ilene Weiss); Rickl, Veronika 16, 44, 53; Sayer, Phil 116, 179–80; Schönborn, Philipp 153, 155; Smith, Roger p.17; Träskclin, Rauno p.181 (left); Tschabold, Mario 26; Ward, David p.15, p.147, p.150, 56–7, 61–2, 84–6, 88–9, 91, 93, 101, 103, 119–20, 159, 161, 171–2, 181–2, 185, 187–9, 196; Watkins, David 30, 117–18, 199; Werkhoven, Ton 208; Whiteside, George 190

We also thank Aspects, British Crafts Centre, Crafts Council, *Crafts* Magazine, Galerie Ra, Galerie Cada, Galerie Mattar, Helen Drutt Gallery.

First published in the United States of America in 1985 by Thames and Hudson Inc.,
500 Fifth Avenue, New York, New York 10110
Revised edition 1994
Library of Congress Catalog Card Number 94-60278
ISBN 0-500-27774-5

Printed and bound in Singapore

CONTENTS

Authors' note

The original edition of this book was compiled by Peter Dormer and Ralph Turner. The text, except for the introduction entitled *The New Jewelry*, was written by Peter Dormer. For this revised edition, Ralph Turner has written the text and selected the illustrations for the new Chapter 4 (*Jewelry and Dissent*) and has also revised the complete *Information* section, beginning on p.201.

THE NEW JEWELRY
A Distinctive Signature

Jewelry is a decorative art and what matters is not the words that can be coined from it, but whether or not it gives pleasure to the wearer and spectator. Most of the works shown in this book are intended to do just that, although people who have not followed developments in jewelry may be surprised at the variety of design and materials now in use.

By the mid-1970s there was abundant evidence of new and exciting work in jewelry, as well as hundreds of art-school-trained professionals displaying considerable expertise – all very different from the situation twenty years earlier, when the number of innovative jewelers throughout Europe and America was small.

Today, we can see the fruits of a dazzling burgeoning of many kinds of ornament, to excite a wide variety of tastes. Some of the new makers have wanted success in the world of fashion, but others have aimed for recognition of a different kind from the world of art. The bid for art status has had several motivations – egotism may be one, but survival is another: art-conscious and design-aware people are more likely customers for the new jewelry. Most important of all, however, jewelers are engaged in a positive reaction against the sort of jewelry generally sold in shops and department stores throughout the Western world.

Most of the jewelry sold by large retailers is conservative in design, mainly because design is often the least important aspect of jewelry which is bought to celebrate or announce an event – an engagement, a wedding, a wedding anniversary. The principal consideration for people buying work for such occasions is that it should look ostentatiously impressive and expensive: this jewelry is a visible, tangible show of affection from one person to another. Much commercial jewelry is therefore designed within a narrow conception of what jewelry ought to look like. And ideas that were once fresh and lively have become clichés. In most commercial jewelry the design matters only as a vehicle for gemstones and precious materials.

Nevertheless, since the Second World War, many craftsmen and craftswomen, particularly in West Germany, have been working in precious materials and have sought to rescue their craft from clichés through good design. For example, the German goldsmith Hubertus von Skal explained his own commitment to goldsmithing by asking a question. Why did early cultures bother to decorate their pots? It was, he said, to give the pots emphasis and distinction, like a signature. And it is the distinctive and the remarkable that Von Skal strives for in his own work. What is curious about commercial jewelry, on the other hand, is its lack of distinctiveness – all the 'signatures' look alike.

West Germany has had an important influence on the development of jewelry. Here the work and teaching of several key masters – notably Hermann Jünger, Friedrich Becker and Reinhold Reiling – has formed the foundation. Jünger, a superb artist in metals, whose experience spans thirty years, has raised the aesthetic aspirations of jewelers whilst promoting high standards of workmanship. His position as Professor of Goldsmithing at the Academy of Fine Arts in Munich and his influential teaching have provided him with an impressive list of former pupils now working in Europe, Australia and America. Becker, from Düsseldorf, has since the 1950s researched into motion and jewelry; he is an expert in kinetic jewelry. Reinhold Reiling, who died in 1983, was professor in the jewelry department of the art school in Pforzheim. Pforzheim is the centre of the jewelry industry in Germany, and has been since the twelfth century. As well as having many workshops and small factories, the town has a unique museum recording the history of jewelry. This Schmuckmuseum (Jewelry Museum) has attracted many craftsmen from all over the world and had an important influence on jewelry in the 1960s and 1970s.

The early 1970s were an adventurous time. Two Germans, Gerd Rothmann and Claus Bury, and an Austrian, Fritz Maierhofer, contributed to an important exhibition in 1971 at the Electrum Gallery, London, which showed for the first time how acrylics could be used creatively. Since then acrylic has become popular with jeweler-designers for its many qualities. It is a rigid material, light, comfortable to wear and, above all, rich in colour. The 1971 exhibition also showed a use of imagery very much of its time, reflecting many of the stratagems of the Pop Art movement in painting.

Claus Bury, in particular, became a major influence, almost a cult figure, admired for his innovative ideas and skilled workmanship. He became fluent in English within a few months as a response to the many invitations he received to teach in England, North America and Australia. Bury's early work combined gold with coloured, translucent acrylic, but in 1975 he began experimenting with non-ferrous metals, eventually finding a way of enriching them with a rich colour palette.

Then he was invited to teach at the Bezalel Academy of Art in Jerusalem, where the desert landscape of light-and-dark contrasts inspired new works – a series of photographs taken of some desert 'sculptures' subsequently became the basis of three-dimensional metal 'drawings'. After these early experiments in Israel, however, it was clear that he would abandon jewelry, and since 1980 he has worked as a sculptor in the United States.

Naturally, there were other German-speaking jewelers whose work was influential in the 1970s, among them the Germans Rüdiger Lorenzen, Norbert Mürrle and Ulrike Bahrs, and the

Above, Ring on plinth. Fritz Maierhofer. Acrylic sheet, gold. 10 cm. Austria, 1973

Above right, First landscape project, Israel. Geometrical Formations, part 1. Claus Bury. Israel, 1975

Right, Diagonal. Claus Bury. Copper, silver, gold. 10.5 cm. West Germany, 1977

Austrians Waltrud Viehböck and Peter Skubic. More recently, serious German jewelers have begun to reconsider the assumptions underlying their work because of the intelligent, sceptical questioning of the Swiss-born jeweler Otto Künzli.

The most noticeable aspect of modern jewelry is the variety of materials used, and in this the Dutch influence has been significant. The history of achievement in modern Dutch jewelry falls into two parts: a highly inventive period from 1965 to the early 1970s, dominated by the rational, radical ware of Emmy van Leersum and Gijs Bakker; then, in 1974, the formation of the B.O.E. group, which rebelled against the rational aesthetic of these jewelers and tried for a freer style, B.O.E. being *Bond van obloerege edeelsmeden* – jewelers in revolt.

Emmy van Leersum and Gijs Bakker had a traditional training in goldsmithing, but both wanted to break with the past. In the mid-1960s, they designed and made a collection of collars and bracelets from aluminum. The use of this material had in part a practical basis, related to its lightness, relative malleability and strength; but it was also a deliberate social-aesthetic choice. The new work was first shown in 1965 at the Galerie Swart in Amsterdam and, the following year, at the Stedelijk Museum. Later in 1966 it transferred to the Ewan Phillips Gallery, London. Significantly, Van Leersum and Bakker have always had a practising interest in industrial design.

Above, Shoulder piece. Gijs Bakker. Blue anodized aluminum. 60 cm. Holland, 1967

Right, Experimental clothing. Emmy van Leersum and Gijs Bakker. Holland, 1971

Bakker in particular has concentrated on work in this field, rather than in jewelry, in recent years. And several young Dutch men and women who have worked in jewelry have followed his example – among them, Frans van Nieuwenborg, Martin Wegman, Marja Staajes and Maria Hees.

In 1969 the Van Leersum/Bakker 'movement' was consolidated in an exhibition in Eindhoven called *Objects to Wear*, which also included work by three other notable jewelry designers – Nicolaas van Beek, Françoise van den Bosch and Bernhard Lameris. One principle common to all was that the jewelry itself had minimal form: the human body became an important part of the jewelry and not just the thing on which it was hung.

In the early 1970s practically everyone in Dutch jewelry (with the exception of Robert Smit) espoused the Van Leersum/Bakker approach, but one woman, Marion Herbst, while acknowledging the achievements of that strong partnership, none the less recognized that there was an alternative. She began her own 'revolution' and formed B.O.E., a group which included Onno Boekhoudt, Françoise van den Bosch (despite, or perhaps because of, her earlier association with the *Objects to Wear* exhibition), Berend Peter and Karel Niehorster. B.O.E. was short-lived, but it succeeded in reacting against the dominant clinical approach. For a while the group, as well as other Dutch jewelers, looked towards Britain, where jewelry design was looser

Bracelet and ring. Marion Herbst.
Chromium-plated copper. 18 cm,
3 cm. Holland, 1971

and freer. Indeed, throughout the 1970s there was a stimulating exchange of ideas between Dutch and British jewelers, with the work of, say, Caroline Broadhead (using tufted nylon and making structures from monofilament) inspiring the use of textiles and colour in Holland. Similarly, David Watkins and Susanna Heron, the British makers, were much impressed by the work of Van Leersum and Bakker.

Although B.O.E. itself did not survive, some of its members, including Herbst and Boekhoudt, have gone on being innovative and influential. Well-designed work, with a restrained expressiveness and colour, has been a characteristic in recent years of other Dutch makers, such as Joke Brakman and Willem Honing. A newcomer, Lam de Wolf, has also made an impact; like Marion Herbst in the 1970s, she may have opened up yet another set of possibilities.

It ought to be noted that many young jewelers, especially in Holland, Britain and the United States, chose to work in non-precious materials to make their work inexpensive. Other designer-jewelers, in the spirit of equality, opted for non-precious materials because they hated the values of wealth, status and power which they thought were wedded to gem-encrusted, precious-metal jewelry.

The extent to which the new jewelry flourishes in Britain is especially interesting. For most of the twentieth century, British jewelry has been overshadowed and influenced by styles and fashions created on the Continent and in Scandinavia. (A deep-rooted misconception still exists in the British public's mind that modern jewelry design stems exclusively from the Scandinavian countries. Undoubtedly the tradition of fine designs there, together with some extensive promotion, has impressed the British market. It is also true that Scandinavia took the lead in exploiting the design market of the 1950s and, as far as jewelry is concerned, the clean, uncluttered lines of Scandinavian work have had a lasting effect on many British makers.)

In the 1950s Gerda Flöckinger, an important designer, was the lone alternative hand in British jewelry. After 1961, when she was appointed head of a new experimental jewelry course at the Hornsey School of Art, the position began to change. Among Flöckinger's pupils have been David Poston and Charlotte de Syllas. Poston was an influential, socially aware jeweler of some significance in the early 1970s (and, as Chapter 1 shows, his work is entering a renewed period of innovation). Charlotte de Syllas follows no trend, but continues to make her own way, producing superbly crafted jewelry of great quality.

For a while, in the 1960s, the British taste was for rough, uncut crystals. Uncut stones are often the preserve of the amateur, but Helga Zahn (born in Germany), in her early work in Britain with pebbles and stones, brought a radical change to jewelry design. Her later pieces, employing agate, were among the most striking jewelry produced before the 1970s. And in an analogous field, another major talent of the period was Patricia Meyerowitz, whose work with machine off-cuts and industrial waste produced surprising and engaging results.

Not many jewelers at this time knew how to get the best out of precious stones, but Peter Hauffé was notable for producing designs that managed to enhance the character of the jewel. And, as a fan of Friedrich Becker, he was one of the few British jewelers to take kinetic jewelry seriously. However, the most successful British jeweler using precious materials imaginatively was Wendy Ramshaw, an important figure in the early 1970s. She remains a leading exponent of

Opposite
Left, Pendant. Patricia Meyerowitz. Silver. 14 cm. UK, 1965

Centre above, Necklace. Helga Zahn. Silver, black pebble. 18 cm.
UK, 1966

Centre below, Set of five gold rings. Wendy Ramshaw. Gold,
inlaid with red enamel. 3.5 cm. UK, 1971

Right, Rings. Gerda Flöckinger. Silver, gold, pearls, garnet. 3.5 cm.
UK, 1967, 1968

This page
Right, Necklace. David Poston. Limestone, hemp, mild steel,
cotton, bronze. 150 cm. UK, 1975

precious-metal jewelry whilst sometimes experimenting with alternative materials and occasionally venturing into performance works.

The 1970s and early 1980s came gradually to be dominated by three names – Susanna Heron, Caroline Broadhead and David Watkins – while a fourth individual – Pierre Degen – is now contributing many new ideas to British jewelry. Others were innovatory, too, including Eric Spiller, Gunilla Treen, Julia Manheim, Catherine Mannheim (who studied with Friedrich Becker), Roger Morris and Tom Saddington.

Looking back, it can be seen that in Susanna Heron and Caroline Broadhead's work certain key forms and ideas stand out as important markers in the development of new British jewelry (although this is not to claim that they are exclusive to Britain). In 1976 Heron produced a collection of acrylic perspex bangles which, for all their simplicity, had character and verve. In 1977 she presented what she called the Jubilee Neckpieces, followed by a range of perspex works taking the theme of the curve, then by quadrangles playing with flat perspectives, by flexible armpieces and by various 'clip on' works. The linking principle, paradoxically, is one of symmetrical asymmetry. In the 1980s her work, with that of Caroline Broadhead and Julia Manheim, developed into 'wearables'. In Heron's case these took the form of 'hats' which were both expressionistic in their use of textiles or paper and minimal in their form – an Oriental quality was now discernible. As Chapter 3 indicates, her work is no longer within the realm of 'jewelry' because her ideas are better realized as sculptures. Caroline Broadhead's inventions of bracelets and necklaces made with tufts of nylon held in a frame of boxwood were very influential – they combined elegance with practicality and simplicity. She too has developed a collection of wearables, some of which are intriguing and idiosyncratic.

David Watkins has digested all the formalist principles of De Stijl, but over a period has produced work which is very much his own – his pieces are often large, highly coloured metal drawings. Of especial interest in his work, and that of Broadhead, Manheim and Heron, is the deliberate designing out of all fastenings, clips and chains which would inhibit and impede the creation of a purist design aesthetic. In terms of abstract composition and colour harmony Watkins, like Eric Spiller, is one of Britain's most mature new jewelry designers.

The influences that have shaped the new jewelry in Europe, especially in Holland and Britain, and with notable contributions from Germany, Austria and Switzerland, have been healthy: a desire to avoid clichés in design; a desire to make exciting, robust and, where possible, cheap ornament; a desire to make jewelry that can be worn by either sex; a frequently expressed distaste for jewelry which is vulgar and merely status-seeking; and always an interest in ensuring that the ornament works with and complements the wearer's body.

It should be an obvious enough point that jewelry is for wearing, but perhaps not that obvious. In the United States, for example, the *current* tendency is to regard jewelry as mini-sculpture rather than wearable ornament which has to be worn in order to be seen properly. Considering again commercial jewelry, we see that much of it has been designed with no thought about how it will work with clothes or move with the body: all manner of objects, from butterflies to vintage cars, perch on lapels or dangle around necks. In Western Europe, by contrast, the major influence in new jewelry is the idea that it must work with the body – a principle that is itself central to the original thinking of Van Leersum and Bakker.

A demonstration of this 'working-with-the-body' doctrine in design can be seen in *The Jewelry Project* (1983) – a selection of modern European work put together by Susanna Heron and a British photographer, David Ward, for the New York collectors Sue and Malcolm Knapp. Some work by Dutch maker Lam de Wolf and Swiss jeweler Pierre Degen takes 'wearability' to 178, p.15 an extreme, and the non-precious materials used include nylon, rubber and polythene. Much of it, however, is discreet and designed to work quietly with the wearer – look, for example, at the pins by Joke Brakman. Such jewelry is designed for clothing and constitutes a simple, elegant 49 ornament which enhances the wearer without overwhelming her or him. It is the epitome of the West European modernist aesthetic, rooted in the German Bauhaus and the Dutch De Stijl, if, at some remove, influenced by the far older spirit of puritanism. Puritan or not, ornament such as this is as much at home on a conventional dress as it is on the tee- or even the hairshirt. Discreet, tasteful ornament can be worn anywhere.

Left, Curved neckpiece. Susanna Heron. Acrylic. 18 cm. UK, 1977

Above, Armband. Pierre Degen. Cloth, wood. 8 cm. UK, 1981

In the development of contemporary European (and American) jewelry, certain individuals who were particularly influential in the 1960s and early 1970s took their initial stance from Bauhaus/De Stijl philosophy but modified it. Emile Souply (Belgium) is an example. Primarily a sculptor, he produced jewelry in the early 1960s that was grounded in Bauhaus teachings: the forms he made were vigorous and undecorated. By 1965 his work had become almost expressionist, making use of gold and baroque pearls. Although Souply is not, currently, a dominant figure in the new jewelry, his earlier work had much merit, not least because it was almost perversely in opposition to new trends.

In Czechoslovakia two important figures have emerged: Svatopluk Kasaly and Anton Cepka. Kasaly was especially innovative in the early 1970s – he used glass, a medium in which the Czechs are expert and creative. His forms are simple and pared down but, though it has something of Emmy van Leersum's rational aesthetic, the work is also warm – a quality it derives from its rhythmic aspect. Anton Cepka's jewelry from the early 1970s is severer and more sculptural. It displays a highly refined sense of colour and draws its imagery from such technology as radar and radio installations, which, as he says, have their own appeal and aesthetic.

In the United States rigorous or pared-down design is currently a less noticeable attribute than in Europe. And it is Americans who remark on the difference. Gary S. Griffin (American metalsmith and sculptor) said about the *International Jewelry Exhibition 1900–1980* (Vienna,

Left, Come Alive, You're in the Pepsi Generation. Brooch. Fred Woell. Copper, brass, steel, glass, photo, silver. 10 cm. USA, 1966

Right, Brothers. Brooch. Robert Ebendorf. Copper, brass, tin, engraved acrylic. 9 cm. USA, 1972

1981, organized by Peter Skubic): 'The European work appeared far more minimal than the American. It represented a design distillation process which resulted in a reductivist aesthetic. Good design and, in most cases, inventive design, [was] an end in itself in the European approach. This was significant when compared to American use of imagery or narrative. Here the hierarchy changed. The image became important; concept displaced the formal elements. The artist's personal philosophy was predominant, not predicated upon a design idea.' (*Metalsmith* magazine, Winter 1981)

In much American work there is a concern with jewelry as separate sculpture, and this strand of American jewelry history goes back to the ideas of the artist Alexander Calder, born in Philadelphia in 1898. Calder, the discoverer of the sculptural mobile, was producing moving constructions powered by motors as early as 1931, though he was soon to discard these mechanical aids to create mobiles which relied upon air currents.

Calder succeeded with jewelry where other painters and sculptors failed (so many have produced watered-down versions of the work they produce in the media that principally interest them). For a while jewelry was an important part of his work. With few tools and none of the apparatus of the conventional jeweler's workshop he handled beaten silver and copper wire with dexterity; spectacular necklaces, bracelets, hair combs and brooches came from his work bench and his first jewelry exhibition was held in late 1940 at the Willard Gallery, New York.

A year after this New York show, the Hungarian-born polymath Moholy-Nagy gave a tutorial at Chicago's School of Design. A jeweler, Margaret de Patta, attended and was very impressed by Moholy-Nagy's ideas. His influence and the Bauhaus philosophy became the core of her

Pendant. Albert Paley. Silver, gold, bronze, pearls, resin. 45 cm. USA, 1972/1973

aesthetic. And one of the significant suggestions she took up was his succinctly expressed exhortation to 'catch the stones in the air, make them float in space – don't enclose them.' An important figure in the prehistory of today's American jewelry, Margaret de Patta died in 1964 before her considerable achievements, especially in the use of the visual properties of gemstones, had been fully acknowledged.

The number of creative jewelers in America today is much greater than elsewhere and the pioneers of these jewelers are also numerous. Without the benefit of tradition or formal training, many jewelers in America learned as they worked, thereby discovering new approaches.

One of the most important trends in American jewelry has been the adoption of assemblage, interest in which was sharpened in 1961 by the exhibition *The Art of Assemblage* held at the Museum of Modern Art in New York. Assemblage in jewelry was anticipated by Sam Kramer, who in 1958 produced a surrealist pendant consisting of traditional materials, together with a yellow and black animal's eye acquired from a taxidermist and set in an ivory mount. Later, during the 1960s the main practitioner of assemblage was Fred Woell, who has relied extensively on found objects.

In the 1960s other influential American jewelers came to the fore or consolidated their positions, among them Arline Fisch, Marjorie Schick, Robert Ebendorf and Stanley Lechtzin. Lechtzin is a well-known goldsmith and one of the first American jewelers to experiment with electroforming. Now an internationally acknowledged master of the technique, he says: 'The control which I exercise over the metal as it grows in the electrolytic solution is a source of stimulation. This process is analogous to numerous growth processes observed in nature and has a considerable meaning to me.' The echo of naturalism, a preference for organic forms, is familiar territory for the crafts and for many people the essence of the wholesome, handmade, craft object, complete with thumb prints. Fortunately, Lechtzin's work is not too obvious or unsubtle in this respect.

Terms such as 'body sculpture', 'sculpture to wear' and 'body art' occur with some frequency in the history of modern American jewelry, notably in the work of Arline Fisch, Nilde Getty, Barry Merritt and Marci Zelmanoff. Although the main innovations in this field are *currently* occurring in Europe, the American Marjorie Schick is undoubtedly one of the most interesting contemporary practitioners of body sculpture. The reasons why body adornment has played such an important role in American jewelry is not clear, but the lack of tradition in conventional jewelry-making must have helped to make Americans receptive to aspects of jewelry not commonly practised. The influence of American Indian culture is one explanation given for the frequent use of feathers and other organic materials and forms. And, added to that, from the 1930s onwards the American experience, especially in New York, has been enriched by European émigrés bringing with them ideas and talents that were sometimes repressed in their homelands. It must also be said that the American talent and demand for spectacle and showmanship are forces much evident in American jewelry.

In much recent American work, there is also (as already noted) interest in jewelry as separate sculpture. Lloyd Herman, Director of the Renwick Gallery, Washington D.C., and organizer of the American exhibition *Good As Gold* (1981), observed: 'One might wonder why creative American jewelers working with the variety of materials evident in *Good As Gold* seem to limit themselves to brooches, necklaces and earrings.' And he provided his own answer. 'It is because brooches are pure form with very little need to function on or fit with the human body; they can be sculptural or decorative, standing alone without the aid of chains, hanging rings, or other fasteners which show and perhaps detract from the originality of their design.' Similarly, Herman went on, earrings and necklaces, although encumbered with chains and clasps, have the same sculptural possibilities of standing alone, but with the added ingredient of movement.

In some ways, the most striking demonstration of the gulf between American and European jewelry in general is Richard Mawdsley's 'Gothic' sculptural work. And yet Janet Koplos, writing in *American Craft* magazine, said, 'Mawdsley is committed to function. He produces pendants, pins and bracelets. One pendant that was too heavy to be worn demonstrates his determination about function: he converted it into a finial for the handle of a ladle.' The Mawdsley piece which has had the most publicity is the Feast Bracelet, an elaborate work which might be satisfactorily viewed as a separate sculpture, but which is in fact worn on the arm. Mawdsley's work is so dominating that the personality of the person who decides to wear one of his pieces is quite as interesting as that of the person who wears one of the *avant-garde* works seen in Chapter 3.

131

Left, Deco Queen. Torso piece. Barry Merritt. Fiberglass, silver, brass, bronze, leather, quartz, agate. 45 cm. USA, 1973

Right, Goldfinger. Bracelet. Bruno Martinazzi. Gold. 9 cm. Italy, 1973

We see a similar play off between jewelry and sculpture in Italy, where several of the important figures in postwar jewelry have been respected sculptors. This is typical of the Italian approach to design and visual aesthetics; their talented designers and artists are not inhibited by artificial barriers between disciplines. In 1967, for example, Gian Montebello began a unique workshop in Milan, inviting sculptors and painters of international standing to design jewelry in collaboration with the Gem Montebello Laboratory. After designs were approved, craftsmen made prototypes for the artists – including Max Ernst, César, Erte, Matta, Niki de Saint Phalle and Lucio Fontana – to approve and correct. Small editions were then made and sold.

Earlier, in the 1950s, the chief exponents of inventive jewelry in Italy were Anton Frühauf (pupil of the sculptor Marino Marini), Mario Pinton and the sculptors Gio and Arnaldo Pomodoro. During the 1960s the Pomodoro brothers were at the height of their inventiveness, with their jewelry and sculpture developing together. Their organic, naturalistic designs intrigued other jewelers in Europe and their influence was especially strong in Britain.

Since the late 1960s, Bruno Martinazzi, well known as a sculptor and jeweler, has used a limited range of images – usually parts of the human body – to create metaphors for various humanitarian ideas (see pls 142–3). His ornament is finely crafted, sensuous without being
47 pornographic. Like a very different, younger Italian jeweler, Giampaolo Babetto, he produces work that is both classical and chic.
37   In the linear jewelry of Italo Antico we can also see the sense of style, apparent ease of conception and flair which is so characteristic of Italian design. Antico is also an important minimalist artist, whose sculpture explores spatial and (through visual metaphor) temporal ideas

which are impossible to pursue in jewelry. Antico, like Martinazzi, Babetto and another interesting jeweler, Francesco Pavan, was active in the 1970s. The work of these makers promises to develop further, although it would be surprising if it followed the radical routes of some of the younger Dutch or British jewelers.

It is clear that the axis of this account, and of this book, is European-American. There is a reason for this, although it will be contested: on the whole, the new jewelry that is produced outside Western Europe and the United States is derivative from it. This state of affairs will not last for very much longer. Developments are taking place elsewhere. In Canada in 1983, for example, Prime Canadian Crafts Gallery in Toronto (run by Suzanne Greenaway) organized a radical exhibition called *Jewelry In Transition*, which was inspired by a London forerunner – *Jewelry Redefined.* Jewelers from all over Canada submitted work to this exhibition and Kai Chan, James   190 Evans and Richard Karpyshin, especially, were noted for their exciting alternatives to traditional   184 jewelry.

Australia's situation is not unlike Canada's: strong ties with Europe and a style of living in some ways reminiscent of the United States. The Crafts Board of the Australian Council has been particularly successful in establishing strong links with organizations in Britain and elsewhere in Europe, resulting in exchanges of exhibitions and special tours. In recent years Australian jewelry has come into its own, with fewer European influences and a greater sense of national identity. A new spirit is emerging that could have exciting repercussions internationally and new Australian jewelers well worth watching include Carlier Makigawa, Marian Hosking, Margaret West and Lyne Tune. Of course, the influences of European teaching continue, and examples of the European schools are to be seen in current Australian work. Hermann Jünger, Claus Bury, David Watkins and Wendy Ramshaw have been key figures and all of them have been visitors to Australia.

Japan is also taking jewelry very seriously, as the International Jewelry Exhibitions in Tokyo have shown. And Israel is producing jewelers of the stature of Esther Knobel. All things considered, the last ten years have been stimulating, with a growth in the number of makers and countries. This expansive, optimistic spirit has made jewelry one of the most exciting activities to practice – and to observe.

EXPRESSION AND DESIGN

*Mainstream
Abstract Jewelry*

Bracelet. Friedrich Becker. Steel. 8 cm. West Germany, 1980

EXPRESSION AND DESIGN
Mainstream Abstract Jewelry

What do we mean by 'mainstream'? Simply this: a glance through the pictures in this section should show that the work is familiar in its function even where the design and materials are novel. The jewelry is usually comfortable and practicable to wear, although clearly, in breaking away from the staleness of department-store ware, it breaches some conventions.

We have left figurative jewelry to the next chapter because its literal, storytelling content demands a different discussion. Here we are concentrating on the abstract and, without sinking too far into the sands of theory, discuss the relative merits of the work on the assumption that no good jewelry or ornament is arbitrary either in its conception or in its manufacture.

A broad distinction between European and American jewelry is drawn in the Introduction, but there are obvious national emphases which reflect differences in design interests and cultural taste within Europe (and, of course, within other countries mentioned in the book, such as Israel, Canada and Australia). Dutch and Swiss work, for example, is generally of a minimalist design: it has an air of puritanism which is not to be found in, say, Italian jewelry. And this holds even for the work by Giampaolo Babetto, the Italian jeweler who has taught at the Rietveld Academy in Amsterdam and has had a strong influence on some young Dutch jewelers. For all its reductivist design, Babetto's work has a measure of chicness which is not characteristic of other Rietveld teachers such as Onno Boekhoudt and Joke Brakman, both of whom are Dutch.

In Germany and Austria we see a greater tendency towards expressionism in jewelry, while the most consistently good British jewelers are design-orientated. Among those already mentioned in the Introduction are Caroline Broadhead and Eric Spiller, Broadhead tending to place an emphasis upon the design idea itself, while Spiller concentrates on the execution of an idea.

On the whole, the young European jewelers are not influenced by particular American makers, although the American contributions to abstract art and certain aspects of design, especially architecture, have been important general influences. Equally, some European jewelers have gone to study and work in America and have found the experience invigorating for their work – Joke van Ommen, from Holland, is a notable example. American jewelry is perhaps closest in spirit to German work in terms of its variety, its concern for technical virtuosity and its occasional hog-stomping brashness. American, German – and Australian –

jewelers are prepared to come down from the wall of obvious good taste (we all know that it is difficult to make De Stijl design look graceless, a fact which, on occasions, makes it a safe, boring option).

The new jewelry tends to fall into one of three categories. First, there is work which is expressive although still highly controlled. Such is the achievement of Hermann Jünger; Robin Quigley (USA); Suzan Rezac (a Swiss resident who trained and now works in the USA); Onno Boekhoudt; and Daniel Kruger (South Africa). The second category veers towards expressionism or exaggeration – it is work which not infrequently has a fetishistic or ritualistic quality about it. Examples here include Beatrix Mahlow (West Germany); Françoise Colpe (Belgium); Bruce Metcalf (USA); Marjorie Schick; and Annie Holdsworth (Australia). Their work does not, however, look alike. Finally, and by far the largest category, there is design-based jewelry. This is where one finds the pretty assemblages of shapes and patterns and where 'simple good taste' tends to rule. Some of the work, nevertheless, can be striking both in its technical virtuosity and in its suitability for a late twentieth-century technological society. Apart from the British jeweler, Eric Spiller, two good makers in the genre are David Tisdale (USA) and Joël Degen (French-born, but he has spent his time as a professional jeweler wholly in England).

It is not practical or necessary to discuss each of the jewelers whose work we have illustrated in this section, but it is right that we should draw out some of the key names. Hermann Jünger and Onno Boekhoudt are two of the most important modern jewelers in Europe, although they are not among the newest faces. The work of both men is expressive. Each manages to touch the emotions, as well as the mind, because his work has a spontaneity and naturalness about it which is akin to the best 'organic' abstract sculpture from the twentieth century, such as that by Brancusi or Moore – which is not to say Jünger or Boekhoudt are making sculptures.

Both men are influential teachers. Among the many important or promising jewelers taught by Jünger at the Munich Academy of Fine Arts have been Daniel Kruger, Miriam Sharlin (USA), Otto Künzli and Manfred Bischoff (West Germany). At the Rietveld Academy, Onno Boekhoudt has taught Joke Brakman, Willem Honing and Annelies Planteydt. All these jewelers we would regard as expressive, although each is different from the others.

1–4   Jünger's work begins with his watercolours and line drawings. The fluency of his drawings cannot be repeated in metal, but can be translated into it; the drawings are for discovering ideas and capturing a spontaneity which would be difficult to attain if all the exploratory work was done through making the jewelry itself. His development owes little to other jewelers, but a great deal to a German painter called Julius Bissier, whose fluid, almost Oriental compositions conveyed an emotional and mental attitude Jünger wanted in his own work.

Expressiveness in Jünger's work derives from two aspects of Bauhaus design – an inclination to keep design to essentials, whilst at the same time incorporating a freer and sometimes more playful ingredient, such as we see in a Paul Klee painting. This combination is also the foundation for other successful modern jewelers, including Robin Quigley. For Quigley also keeps her designs reduced and allows a playful and magical element (one deliberately reminiscent of Kandinsky) to come to the fore.

29–32

It is important that there is no attempt to force the design or the playfulness, thus emphasizing the importance of spontaneity. Spontaneity in this context is not random or uncontrolled gesture, but a fluency of expression which demands at least two ingredients – a skill, a dexterity, which is more or less second nature and is a natural tool to the maker's imagination; and a clear idea of where the design could go.

Jünger has a varied and extensive vocabulary of shapes and images, which has an affinity with both natural or found objects and with the ritual devices or tools of fifty centuries ago. In one sense his influence among younger German jewelers must be rather restrictive: since he has such a wide repertoire, his work offers rich pickings for plagiarists, and the young, having no voice of their own, tend to plagiarize. Yet Jünger is not alone in West Germany in the diversity of his work. Daniel Kruger is currently one of the most innovative of makers, and among the newest jewelers Manfred Bischoff, Justine Wein and others are finding their own voices.

Onno Boekhoudt's work is different. It is in the spirit of the De Stijl movement, but that is not quite the whole truth. The art historian Hans Jaffé pithily describes the secret of De Stijl as lying 'in the fundamental principle of its philosophy, in the concept of harmony and the suppression of individualism'. Harmony, yes – but lack of individualism is not a feature of Boekhoudt's work.

Boekhoudt's jewelry is not geometrical; it retains a natural quality which comes from keeping some of the attractiveness that worked metal has just before its edges and surfaces are finally honed up and polished. In his recent work, Boekhoudt has been making small collections of objects in which only one item in each collection is to be worn; the other items are fetishistic, and so, by association, is the jewelry.

5–6

Simplicity does not preclude expressiveness. And the work of Boekhoudt's former students – such as Brakman, Planteydt and Honing – although simple in design, also has a rightness, a touch of fluent gesture that can be found in something like calligraphy, too. Willem Honing explains himself as follows:

In my work it is important that the material will reveal itself in terms of what it is capable of doing. Perspex being translucent and opaque, papier-mâché being both flexible and stiff with a rough or smooth surface, and tar-paper being very pliable. However, it is not these material qualities which provide the starting-points for my jewelry. I begin with a certain feeling that I want to create and according to this feeling I arrange the elements which make the piece.

Simple expressiveness is not the preserve of Europeans. Robin Quigley aside, there are other Americans and American-trained jewelers, such as Miriam Sharlin and Suzan Rezac, whose

Brooches. Justine Wein. Silver. 6 cm (largest). West Germany, 1981, 1982

10, 54 work is both expressive and discreet. Suzan Rezac's work is 'of its time', being an amalgam of metalsmithing skills and decorative devices adapted from twentieth-century abstract painting. The combination of such metals as silver, nickel, gold and copper gives her work a muted richness which goes well with the soft-edged geometry of the forms – a very touchable art. The overtures to abstract painting are seen elsewhere in American work, and the enamel brooches by Jamie Bennett, for example, are abstract 'paintings' made small.

In considering the expressionist category it is worth noting that, almost perversely, reductivist design can sometimes enter the range of exaggerated gesture. An example of this is Gabriele 57 Dziuba's (West German) 'Z' pin. And there is also the work of the American maker, Marjorie Schick. Although we illustrate her work in Chapter 3, her more practical ornament has a place in mainstream simply because it is attractive and lively and, if on the large size, not so outrageous that it turns the wearer into a performance piece. She says, 'I consider my painted wood pieces as sculptural "stick" drawings to wear' and hopes that each piece, through the process of making, 'will retain an element of spontaneity and liveliness'. The work is expressionist 198 and has a tribal or ritual quality which, as we see in Chapter 3, gets taken to extremes.

Expressionism usually takes more elaborate forms than it does in the work of Dziuba and 11, 12 Schick. Consider Beatrix Mahlow. The components of her jewelry – which is very finely made – resemble the artefacts found in ethnographical collections, such as axe heads, blades, tribal 'objects'. For most of us such ornaments and artefacts mean very little because we do not know their function or their context. Yet it is partly because of our ignorance that they encourage our curiosity, the more so if they are well made and interestingly decorated. Such qualities apply to Mahlow's work. Together with her materials – a combination of the metaphor-sustaining metals like gold and silver, and the translucent rigidity of plastic – it makes up a puzzling and frequently rather beautiful range of ornament. Consistent with the European 'tradition', Mahlow's work also takes on a new life and a coherence when it is worn.

Equally expressionist in a blunter, more direct way, is Friedrich Müller (West Germany), whose 26
simple brooches of twisted metal have more artifice about them than first meets the eye. He
explains that he is 'fascinated by the process which is imposed on materials' and what he has
done is simply to apply basic shaping to the bars of metal in order that 'the real value and the
actual nature of the metal may be divined'.

Expressionism in modern jewelry is a characteristic of American work. This is not surprising
given the nature of American design in daily life – in advertising, packaging and cars, and in
office and hotel lobbies. It is equally no surprise that the trend in architecture toward eclectic
decoration ('Post-Modernism' or 'Ornamentalism') is in its most interesting, exciting and
eccentric forms in the USA. One of the most lively commentators on American design – a man
who also pulls the rug out from under the arrogant feet of the European minimalist designers – is
Tom Wolfe. As he observes in *From Bauhaus to Our House*, this is the American century: 'This is
the century when America became the richest nation in all of history, with a wealth that reached
down to every level of the population. The energies and animal appetites and idle pleasures of
even the working classes – the very term now seemed antique – became enormous, lurid,
creamy, preposterous.'

Of course, Tom Wolfe's prose is lurid and creamy in its exaggeration and yet it rings
sufficiently true to explain why Holland and not the USA might be the home of 'quiet' jewelry.
Even the most basic geometrical work in America, such as Ann Scott's neckpieces, is bolder in its
geometry and patterning than anything in Europe which might remotely be considered as an
equivalent. Even where the work is really a matter of anodizing metals and shaping them into
bracelets, the American maker tends to want to express the geometry of the geometry.

These cultural influences have interesting consequences. We have already remarked on the
fact that America has had an impact on the Dutch maker Joke van Ommen, just as Miriam 74
Sharlin (USA) has been influenced by West German jewelers during her studies in Munich. Van
Ommen says: 'Although function is my starting point in my thinking, it is definitely not all. Of
course I want to make beautiful pieces as well. Lately a change has taken place in my work (due
to my move to Washington?) – it has become more three-dimensional. I experiment with
different materials, like mother of pearl, shells, ivory.' This change does not mean a change for
the worse in Van Ommen's work, though purists might cry for function and simplicity and might
gulp at the 'creamy' materials. It is, indeed, interesting that Van Ommen is responding to what is
an apparent feature in American design – the feeling that anything is permitted.

We might also argue that American work challenges a particular European orthodoxy that
development should be evolutionary, slow and rational. Who needs rational jewelry? Probably
not David LaPlantz, American jeweler and Art Professor at Humboldt State University,
California. LaPlantz is a success. Alan Revere, jewelry designer, has written: 'Praised by *The New*

Neckpiece. Ann Scott. Acrylic, silver, steel.
22 × 22 × 2 cm. USA, 1982

70, 72   *York Times, Los Angeles Times* and *Ornament* Magazine, LaPlantz's new collection is a visual treasure chest. . . . The work is bold, vibrant, intriguing, and wearable. It represents the total commitment of a vital and exuberant artist . . . He has set out to retain the originality and uniqueness of his previous work [metal containers], however, and the jewelry is totally spontaneous. Perhaps a sketch or two, and then off he goes into the metal, to play out living dreams in anodized technicolor.' Currently, LaPlantz works in anodized or painted aluminum, creating vivid colours into which he engraves, so that the lines show through as silver. The works are constructions – 'miniature art forms' – and clearly stand on their own when not being worn. This is wearable art but not based on wearability. After two years of making jewelry proper (but after a longer period as a metalsmith), LaPlantz has work in most of the important public and private modern collections.

In one sense, LaPlantz is an epitome of an American ideal which manages to combine competitiveness, ambition, ego and energy with the belief that life should be lived with *wholesome* enjoyment – or, to quote from his statement of intent, 'I feel very lucky to be doing what I am doing both as an artist and teacher [twice voted at his University as its most Outstanding Professor of the Year] – both pay dividends that are worth more than gold – a satisfaction, a peace, a reason to smile and arise each dawn.' And although many European jewelers would sniffily dismiss all this as somehow not quite respectable or appropriate for the serious artist, there are others who would agree. Who needs an angst-ridden jeweler?

LaPlantz explains that his work is instinctive: 'I'm not aware of some of the things that are happening with the lines until after I am done. It's like you do the work and then afterwards say, well that's pretty nice.' He makes very few drawings and favours spontaneity, which is also a feature of his teaching: he gives his students problems that have to be solved within three hours.

'The decisions are not "can I or can't I", it's "yes", "no". It's like making a split-timing decision. If someone throws an axe at you, you have to do something. You have to respond. If it's wrong, it's wrong but then your next decision kind of corrects for that.'

The purpose of labouring LaPlantz's work and ideas is partly because of the rapid importance he appears to be achieving in the American modern jewelry world and partly because emphasis upon quickness, hard work and continuous change appears to be as much a feature of American work as caution and reductivism are among Europeans. There is certainly a critical distinction over the matter of spontaneity. LaPlantz's analogy of the hurled axe would not strike many teachers in German or Dutch art colleges as particularly appropriate. Much European art teaching is still very strongly rooted in the Bauhaus and especially in the spirit of the approach set out by the Swiss teacher, Johannes Itten. A brief paragraph, very much on the theme of spontaneity and taken from his book *Design and Form*, makes the point: 'A fern was studied for half an hour every morning during one week to grasp and understand the movements of its characteristic form. On the last day the fern pot was put aside, and the drawing was produced in a single emotion within fifteen minutes.'

The sort of spontaneity that LaPlantz epitomizes is different in kind from that of Jünger, Kruger, Quigley and the minimalist Europeans such as Johanna Hess-Dahm, Annelies Planteydt and Joke Brakman. They aspire more to the spontaneity found in Chinese calligraphy, where a stroke is quick and fluent but owes its spontaneity to a great deal of knowledge. Very few new jewelers worldwide have this ability.

A comparison can be made with expressionist painting, although it is a little misleading in the sense that there is little scope in LaPlantz's work, or that of any jeweler, for free gesture. Nevertheless, the quickness of design and manufacture, and the possibility of any one of several 'answers' being satisfactory, makes such a parallel tolerable. LaPlantz is an honest teacher and possibly a useful corrective to the unnecessarily rigid approach of some Europeans. He says, 'When answering a question, I will give at least five or six possible solutions to the problem in a piece. . . . So often teachers act like Gods with the one and only "true" answer.'

Work produced in this way may be attractive, but it is also true that such an approach is the dominant one in the second league of new jewelry throughout the West. The very best work has a look of 'necessity' about it – a suggestion that to alter the form or modify the decoration would be to make that piece weaker. One of the pitfalls of expressionism is its arbitrariness – and abstract expressionism, whether in jewelry, applied decoration to a building, sculpture or painting, may let you down, merely getting by through being tastefully random.

Expressionism of a different sort in American jewelry, one with obvious sculptural content, is apparent in Bruce Metcalf's work, which is more often table sculpture than wearable jewelry. 139–41 Metcalf has a wide vocabulary of forms and shapes which are largely organic, highly animated and very ambiguous. Even the abstract work somehow manages to suggest a succession of comic-strip cartoons. His pieces certainly entertain the mind because they are richly fetishistic, and all manner of scatological, sexual and violent references might emerge from these curious fantasies.

The ambition towards jewelry as sculpture, whether expressionist or not, usually takes one of the two forms outlined in the Introduction. There is the approach of makers such as Metcalf, in which the piece is seen as an autonomous object, and there is work which uses the person wearing it as a part of an overall body sculpture. Some makers try to do both. They try to make objects that can stand on their own as interesting autonomous artefacts and that also have another 'life' when worn: a difficult ambition to secure. David Selkirk (Western Australia) says that his recent 'solid pieces echo the form and line of the body but although fitting it sympathetically they have a presence independent of the body, functioning alone as objects'.

It is not hard to sympathize with the jeweler wanting to extend the expressive qualities of his or her work into the period when it is not worn – to treat it as sculpture, rather than a fashion accessory spending most of its time in a drawer. But really rather little of the jewelry that is designed to have a separate aesthetic life is worthy of the title 'sculpture'; it belongs more readily to the category of domestic ornament – the category occupied by most ceramic- and glassware, with its function being to decorate and to distract. (Arguably, a lot of work that is called 'sculpture' is in the same category.) This implies a constraint – one resented by more ambitious makers – for jewelry to be well mannered, deferring to the fact that it is to be worn by someone or live in someone's house. What suits the gallery need not suit the function of personal adornment and domestic decoration. At the same time, if the point of testing limitations is in fact to make more interesting, innovative and wearable work, then such questioning is not only healthy but necessary. One consistently thoughtful jeweler in this regard is David Watkins. His work has progressed naturally over a ten-year period, marked always by very fine craftsmanship and an excellent sense of colour. During this decade he has taken excursions into body sculpture and the results have fed back into his functional ware. In other words, he has not fallen to the temptation to make arbitrary, large-scale performance pieces just for the sake of being different. In many respects, his new geometrical work, whilst it is clearly unconventional, is none the less well within any recognized definition and practice of jewelry.

Makers do talk about their work 'making a statement', but they have borrowed the jargon from fine artists, most of whom are equally at a loss, if pressed, to indicate what the content of such a statement might mean. Notwithstanding its expressive and expressionist capacities, most of the new jewelry is simple design, though not necessarily the worse for that.

To devise ornament and design that will stay fresh is clearly difficult, especially since staying fresh is not to be confused with fashion. Much good ornament from the Arts and Crafts

78

117–18
170, 199

Double triangle. Neckpiece. David Watkins.
Steel, with yellow gold. 45 cm. UK, 1978

Movement, Jugendstil, Art Nouveau and Art Deco has passed in and out of fashion, but has always been recognized as good ornament. Indeed, the rapidity with which 'movements' are rediscovered might make one suspect that the last decade has not been a fertile period for inventive ornament. We think otherwise. There has certainly been some purely 'design'-based new jewelry which has a perfection of pattern about it which makes it continuously pleasing. Such work tends not to 'express' anything other than how it is to be worn, and mostly not even that: it simply 'is'. People to single out here include Eric Spiller, Caroline Broadhead, Paul Derrez (Holland), Nora Fok (Hong Kong), Therese Hilbert (Switzerland), Frank Bauer (West Germany), Jean-Paul Aleman (France), Joël Degen and David Tisdale.

Their work is demonstrably clever. Caroline Broadhead's idea of simply pushing one's hand (or head) through tufts of coloured nylon or cotton was almost laughably simple, but it has produced ornament which is both elegant and pretty. Mecky van den Brink's jewelry at the beginning of the 1980s is a good example of the Broadhead influence, as is Nora Fok's. Nora Fok, however, prefers to use colour and form with delicacy and restraint. 101

Paul Derrez's work also has about it a quality of reserve – it is rational design without being inhuman, and, like quite a lot of Dutch work, is reminiscent of traditional Dutch dress; his 'neckpieces' have as their antecedents the beautiful, large ruffs of 17th-century Dutch dress. Derrez, commenting on why he had selected a particular work for the *Jewelry Redefined* show in 120

London (1982), gave an explanation of his own values in jewelry. 'For me this piece is original, humorous and clever. It has logical shape which shows how to fasten it. The opposing materials give it a powerful contrast, and both men and women can wear it without any connotations of luxury, wealth and status. This is exactly my approach to jewelry.'

Making work that is properly of its own time is not so easy. We know that this is the age of technology and that the best craftsmanship and design is to be found in the aircraft, space and communications industries. Yet a straightforward lifting of technological imagery would not lead to good ornament. On the other hand, if the spirit of technology's perfection can be taken
113 as a starting point, then the results can be very good. Eric Spiller's work is an example. Much of it is not simple; it has been mathematically worked out and meticulously executed and machine-tooled. Nothing is left to chance. But an element of that precious 'spontaneity', which has surfaced so many times in this chapter, is present because he makes use of chance-effects of light as the object moves when it is worn. Edward de Large, who was born in Britain but lives in the USA, also captures the spirit of technology and he has had an important influence in America through his research into anodizing titanium.

Some design-based jewelry takes its cue from expressing its function and this is a feature of
75 David Tisdale's work. Tisdale's work is characteristically American in that it can stand on its own as autonomous ornament, unlike (for example) the much simpler work of the Dutch jeweler,
76 Coen Mulder, which is otherwise similar in materials and function. Mulder's work comes alive only when worn. And Tisdale is almost expressionistic in making his design speak its function. His bangle, for example, exaggerates the function of enclosing the wrist into a piece of engineering; its construction has been strongly emphasized.

Frank Bauer is one who lies between the soft-edge designers, such as Broadhead and Fok, and
17 the machine-aesthetic designers, such as Spiller and Tisdale. Bauer has moved on from his beautifully made intricate gold structures (mostly pendants and brooches) to pins with rubber
116 thread. These are very simple and cling to the clothing like burrs: an elegant design.

The only constraints on design in new jewelry are straightforward practical ones and even these can be broken if wearers can be persuaded to co-operate. Yet there have been surprisingly few adventures outside geometry. In the figurative section, there are some innovative designs from, for example, Manfred Bischoff, but the new jewelers in Europe tend to keep their designs controlled and plain. There is, perhaps, a lack of confidence among most of the younger jewelers in making patterns.

In one way the new jewelers have spared themselves the effort and the need for 'decorating' their work because their materials frequently offer a range of colours and abstract patterns built in. For example, there is a variety of plastics which are manufactured in order to catch the light and break it into rainbow colours; there are also many different kinds of foil, coloured yarns and coated papers which are inherently pretty and well suited to the 'cut and fold' geometries favoured by many of the younger jewelers. It is almost tempting to say that the alternative materials have been less flexible in some respects than the traditional ones. For where there is a need to beat, hammer and forge there also develops the desire to experiment and force the material to its limits. This is the route to surprise. On the other hand, when the limitations of the material are apparent and the colour and even the pattern are 'given', then cutting and folding is all that is left: innovation is dependent only upon novel assemblage techniques.

Sometimes what is missed is the pleasure of good workmanship. All design and ornament can be undermined by bad workmanship, as we know. But there have been occasions during the last ten years or so when it has been fashionable to set 'craft' on one side on the assumption that 'craft' is boring and plodding and somehow prevents the Phoenix of creativity from rising. What has happened is that the Phoenix has turned into an Icarus. Workmanship has been treated with disdain in some quarters as though it were an attribute which anyone could easily attain for themselves. The most familiar attack on craftsmanship has been that an overemphasis on technique kills the spontaneity of a design. Certainly an overworking of materials can damage the look of an object; it is possible to over-polish, overdo the crispness of an edge, dull a colour or have an altogether over-finished look to a design. But overworking is bad craftsmanship. We are concerned with appropriate workmanship. David Poston, the British jeweler, has decided in his new work that the design requires a certain looseness of finish, he wants to retain a flavour of what the metal looks like when it is being worked. This is good. It is not carelessness; it is not a matter of whamming something together for a quick effect.

Good workmanship has to be as much a feature of working non-precious metals as it is of gold and silver. In some cases there has been a laxness about quality, but the trend is currently firmly against this – it is a part of the spirit of the 1980s that a concern for quality of manufacture and design is uppermost in the purchaser's, as well as the maker's, mind.

121

Opposite 1 Pendants and brooch. Hermann Jünger.
Gold, silver. 4–10 cm. West Germany, 1980

2 Two necklaces
   Hermann Jünger
   Gold, silver
   60 cm, 50 cm
   West Germany, 1980

3 Pendants
   Hermann Jünger
   Gold, silver, enamel
   4.5–14.5 cm
   West Germany, 1978, 1979

4 Pendants
   Hermann Jünger
   Gold, silver, agates
   7 cm
   West Germany, 1981

5 Rings with objects
Onno Boekhoudt
Silver, copper, steel
2–10 cm
Holland, 1983

6 Armband with objects
Onno Boekhoudt
Silver, copper, lead
10 cm
Holland, 1983

7 Necklace, earrings
Daniel Kruger
Silver
18 cm d, 4 cm d
West Germany, 1983

8 Necklace
  Daniel Kruger
  Silver, thread, glass beads
  18 cm d
  West Germany, 1975

9 Two brooches
  Miriam Sharlin
  Silver, copper, stainless steel
  8 × 7 cm
  USA, 1982

10 Bracelet
   Suzan Rezac
   Silver
   11 cm
   USA, 1983

11 Wearable objects/pendants
    Beatrix Mahlow
    Silver, gold-coloured metals
    12–24 cm
    UK/West Germany, 1982

12 Neckpiece
    Beatrix Mahlow
    Painted metal, etched acrylic
    24 cm
    UK/West Germany, 1982

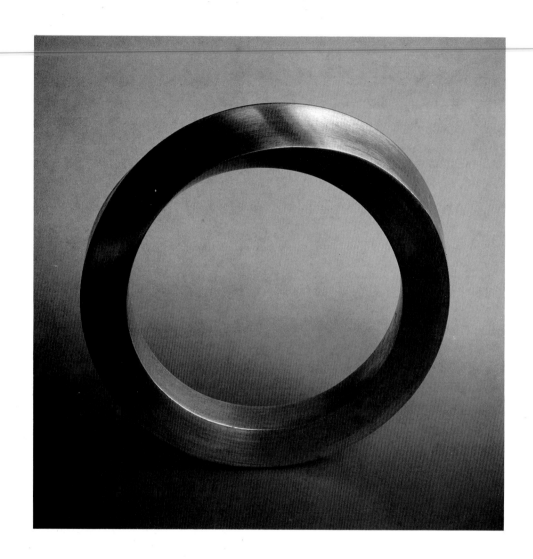

13 Bracelet
    Gijs Bakker
    Aluminum
    9 cm
    Holland, 1968

14 Bracelet for
        the upper arm
    Willem Honing
    Sawn perspex
    10.4 cm
    Holland, 1981

15 Bracelet for
        the upper arm
    Willem Honing
    Sawn perspex
    14 cm
    Holland, 1981

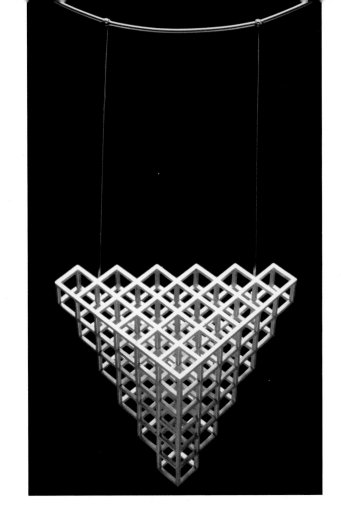

16 Pins
   Rita Grosse-Ruyken
   Forged gold
   22 × 9 cm
   West Germany, 1977

17 Pendant
   Frank Bauer
   Gold
   20 cm h
   West Germany/UK, 1980

18 Necklace
   Annelies Planteydt
   Gold
   15 cm
   Holland, 1983

19 Necklace
   Caroline Strieb
   Gold, ivory
   15 cm
   USA, 1983

20 Earrings
   Holly Belsher
   Gilding metal, steel
   5 cm h
   UK, 1981

21 Earrings
   Cornelia Ratting
   Gold, steel
   5 × 3.5 cm
   UK, 1982

22, 23
Brooches
Jan Wehrens
Gold
5 cm, 10 cm
West Germany, 1980, 1981

24 Set of four pins
Wendy Ramshaw
Gold, black basalt,
 opal, moonstone
12, 14, 12, 14 cm
UK, 1981

25 Three brooches
  Doris Sacher
  Gold, silver
  14 cm
  West Germany, 1981

26 Brooch
  Friedrich Müller
  Brass, steel
  7 cm
  West Germany, 1982

27 Bracelet
  Annette Rössle
  Copper, gold
  12 cm
  West Germany, 1978

28 Bracelet
  Daniel Kruger
  Silver
  7 cm
  West Germany, 1982

29–32
Four brooches
Robin Quigley
Silver, epoxy resin
6.25 cm
USA, 1982

33 Bracelet
Annie Holdsworth
Acrylic, silver
9 cm
Australia, 1982

34 Brooch
   Jamie Bennett
   Enamel, silver
   5 cm
   USA, 1979

35 Rectangular pattern bracelet
   David Tisdale
   Anodized aluminum, silver, onyx
   7 × 3 × 5.5 cm
   USA, 1983

36 Brooch
   Helen Shirk
   Silver, titanium, gold
   7.5 cm
   USA, 1982

37 Necklace
   Italo Antico
   Silver
   32 cm
   Italy, 1976

38 Four bracelets
    Helen Aitken-Kuhnen
    Silver (sandblasted), enamel
    7 cm
    Australia, 1983

39 Bangle, ring, both with
        interchangeable heads
    Paul Derrez
    Silver, perspex
    6 cm, 2 cm
    Holland, 1977

40 Bracelets
    Ben Wisman
    Acrylic with steel balls
    12 cm
    Holland, 1982

41 Brooches
   Elisabeth Holder
   Steel, silver
   5 cm
   UK, 1980

42 Rings
   Giorgio Cechetto
   Silver
   2.5 cm
   Italy, 1983

43 Rings
   Wilhelm Mattar
   Silver
   2 cm
   West Germany, 1982

44 Désir extraterrestre
   Brooch, model for sculpture
   Rita Grosse-Ruyken
   Forged gold
   22 × 9 cm
   West Germany, 1982

45 Pendants
Johannes Kuhnen
Anodized aluminum, silver
8 cm
Australia, 1983

46 Brooches
Elisabeth Holder
Copper, gold, steel
7.5 cm, 4 cm
UK, 1980

47 Rings
Giampaolo Babetto
Silver, gold, resin
5 cm
Italy, 1983

48 Bracelet, necklace
Joelle Levie
Plexiglass
7 cm, 14 cm
Belgium, 1983

49 Pins
Joke Brakman
Acrylic, steel
7 cm
Holland, 1982

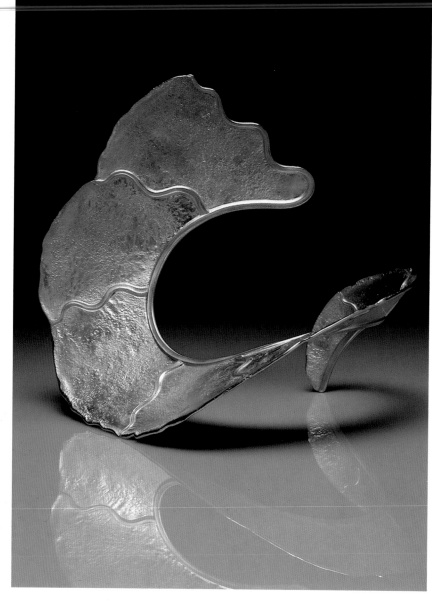

50 Ring
Yehuda Tiglat
Gold
5 cm
Israel, 1980

51 Bracelet
Jackie Mina
Gold
8 cm
UK, 1980

52 Necklace
E.R. Nele
Gold, silver, pearls
18 cm
West Germany, 1983

53 Necklaces
Rita Grosse-Ruyken
Forged gold
34–35 cm (pendants 5 cm)
West Germany, 1979

54 Necklace
    Suzan Rezac
    Silver, gold, nickel, copper
    18 cm
    USA, 1983

55 Pins
    Annie Holdsworth
    Gold, perspex, slate, brass, steel
    9 cm
    Australia, 1983

56 Push-through pins
Johanna Hess-Dahm
Anodized aluminum
12 cm
Switzerland, 1982

57 Z pin
Brooch
Gabriele Dziuba
Painted wood
15 cm
West Germany, 1982

58 Cuboid
Armpiece
George Dobler
Painted steel
$8 \times 6 \times 3$ cm
West Germany, 1982

59 Neckpiece, body ornament
Therese Hilbert
Steel
20–50 cm, flexible
West Germany, 1983

60 Neckpiece
Herman Hermsen
Painted steel
25 cm
Holland, 1982

61 Wisp
  Armpiece
  Nora Fok
  Dyed nylon
  15 cm h
  Hong Kong, 1981,
    1982

62 Armpiece
  Nora Fok
  Dyed nylon
  14 cm h
  Hong Kong, 1981

63 Silver rib
  Bracelet
  Arline Fisch
  Knitted silver
  14 cm h
  USA, 1983

Overleaf
64 Brooches, rings, earrings
  Top left, then clockwise:
  Louise Slater, Paul Derrez,
  Cathy Harris, Louise Slater,
  Cathy Harris, Cathy Harris
  Acrylic, plastic coated
    paper, steel
  17 cm (largest)
  Derrez, Holland, 1981
  Harris/Slater, UK, 1983

65 Brooches, necklace
  Peter Niczewski
  Marquetry – natural,
    dyed wood veneers
    on plywood
  9 cm, 35 cm
  UK, 1982

66 Pendant
   Alain Lerolle
   Titanium, aluminium, resins,
   emerald
   8 cm
   France, 1985

67 Brooch
   Chavent
   Silver, gold
   10 cm
   France, 1985

68 Earrings, bangle and rings
   Raphaelle Gautier
   Acrylic, ebony
   4 cm, 10 cm, 2.5 cm
   France, 1983

69 Neckpiece
   Therese Hilbert
   Steel, brass
   28 × 45 cm
   West Germany, 1983

70 Bracelet
   David LaPlantz
   Aluminum, ribbon wire
   8.5 cm
   USA, 1983

71 Brooch
   David LaPlantz
   Aluminum
   8.5 cm
   USA, 1983

72 Pins
   George Dobler
   Steel, epoxy-covered wire
   22 cm (longest)
   West Germany, 1983

73 Brooch
   Edward de Large
   Titanium, silver
   5 cm h
   UK, 1976

74 Kite
   Brooch
   Joke van Ommen
   Anodized aluminum
   7 cm
   USA, 1983

75 Bangle, earrings
   David Tisdale
   Anodized aluminum
   4 cm, 9 cm
   USA, 1983

76 Three bracelets and pin
   Coen Mulder
   Anodized aluminum
   10 cm
   Holland, 1983

77, 79
   Brooches
   Johanna Hess-Dahm
   Painted wood
   15 cm
   Switzerland, 1983

78 Two brooches
   David Selkirk
   Silver, copper, nickel
   7 cm
   Australia, 1983

80 Neckpiece
Belinda Ross
Epoxy resin, acrylic
22 cm
UK, 1983

81 Torque no 68
Pendant
Stanley Lechtzin
Silver, silver gilt, amethyst
38 × 17 × 28 cm
USA, 1983

82 Bracelets
Cathy Wren (bottom)
Louise Slater (top)
Plastic, acrylic
10 cm
UK, 1983

83 Necklace
   Louise Sant
   Brass mesh, silver,
     silver wire
   15 cm
   UK, 1981

84 Necklace
   Françoise Colpe
   Cotton, wool, feather,
     stainless steel
   25 cm
   Belgium, 1982

85 Looped cord earrings
   Annie Sherburne
   Silk, rayon, cord
   10 cm
   UK, 1982

86 Bracelet
   Lisa Gralnick
   Enamel on copper,
     ivory, feathers,
     metallic thread
   20 cm extended
   USA, 1982

87 Brooch
   Marion Herbst
   Iron
   14 cm
   Holland, 1980

88 Necklace
   Mecky van den Brink
   Cotton
   25 cm
   Holland, 1983

89 Bracelets
   Beppe Kessler
   Rubber bands
   10 cm
   Holland, 1982

90 Armbands
   Willem Honing
   Papier-mâché
   11 cm h
   Holland, 1982

92 Pins
   Marlies Bächinger,
   Alban Hürlimann,
   Katharina Issler
   Rubber, brass pins
   2–3 cm
   Switzerland, 1982

93 Bracelets
   Emmy van Leersum
   Laminated PVC,
      coloured paper
   12 cm h
   Holland, 1982

94 Brooch
   Marion Herbst
   Woven textile
   10 cm
   Holland, 1979

95 Necklaces
   Mecky van den Brink
   Knitted transparent nylon,
      dyed nylon
   15 cm
   Holland, 1982

96 Bracelets
   Maria Hees
   Leather
   10 cm
   Holland, 1983

97 Neckpiece
   Caroline Broadhead
   Wood hoop, dyed nylon
      tufts
   20.5 cm (hoop)
   UK, 1981

98, 99
Bracelet, earrings
Rena Koopman
Coloured golds
 (sandblasted)
7 cm, 5 cm
USA, 1980, 1981

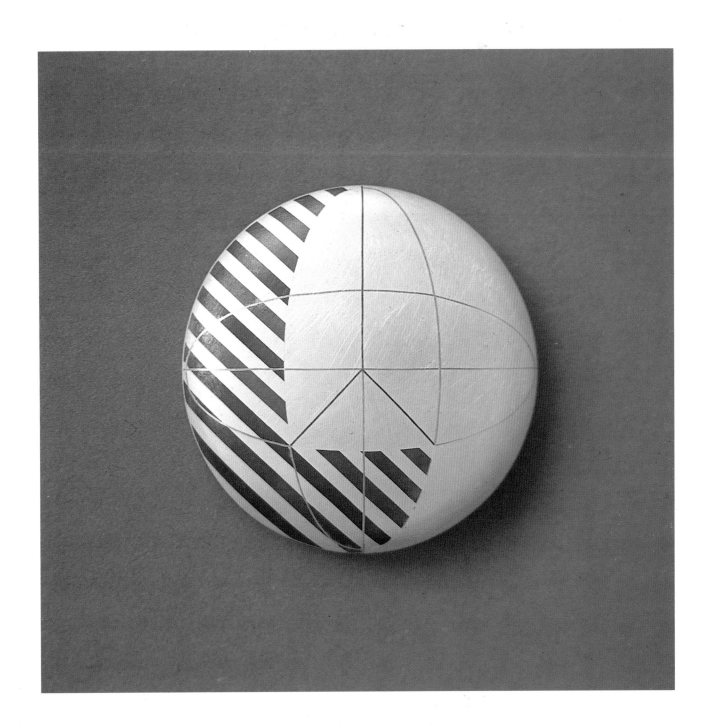

100 Brooch
Fritz Maierhofer
Silver, gold
6 cm d
Austria, 1977

101 Three armpieces
(left–right) Eric Spiller,
Caroline Broadhead,
Susanna Heron
Aluminum, wood, nylon,
  perspex
7–8 cm d
UK, c. 1980

102 Brooches
Charon Kranson
Steel, thread
5 cm, 8 cm, UK, 1983
Bracelet
Herman Hermsen
Steel
8 cm, Holland, 1982

103 Neckpiece
Barbara Alcock
Textile, steel
18 cm
UK, 1982, 1983

104 Bracelet
   Hans Georg Pesch
   Silver, titanium
   9.5 cm
   West Germany,
      1983

105 Bracelet
   Friedrich Becker
   White gold,
      emerald
   7 cm
   West Germany,
      1980

Joël degen
spring 1978

round 3 points diamond

stainless steel screws : 16

18 ct yellow/white gold

anodised titanium

18 ct white gold

12 14 points diamonds

anodised titanium

stainless steel screw

stainless steel washer
3

stainless steel ball-bearing

18 ct yellow/white gold

6 stainless steel screws

anodised titanium
18 ct yellow/white gold

anodised titanium
6 stainless steel screws

'worry ring' consisting of a
revolving cylinder attached to
the shank by means of a
shielded ball bearing.
12 baguette diamonds are
arranged around the cylinder
and held in place by means
of titanium discs.
the ball-bearing is positioned
inside the cylinder between —
above — a tubular structure
into which is set a round
diamond — underneath — a
disc with 12 tapped holes which
receive the 12 screws which hold
the whole structure together.
the ball-bearing is secured to
the shank around a shaft with
a screw and washer.
the gold shank is faced on
either side with titanium discs
fastened to it by screws.

106 Ring drawings
Joël Degen
UK, 1978

107 Bangle
Benny Bronstein
Steel sheet, cable
8 cm
Israel, 1980

108 Bangle
Joël Degen
Anodized aluminum
7 cm
UK, 1982

109, 110
Kinetic rings
Friedrich Becker
Steel
3 cm
West Germany, 1980

111 Bracelets
   Caroline Broadhead
   Nylon
   14 cm
   UK, 1981

112 Ring, brooch, earrings,
      bracelet
   Daphne Krinos
   Pearl, gold, anodized
      metals
   8 cm (largest)
   UK, c. 1983

113 Brooches, bangles
   Eric Spiller
   Anodized aluminum
   3–7 cm
   UK, 1980, 1981

114 Brooches
Ben Wisman
Aluminum, steel
10 cm
Holland, 1982

115 ZigZag brooches
Carlier Makigawa
Brass, silver,
enamel paint
6.3 × 4 cm
Australia, 1983

116 Pins
Frank Bauer
Rubber, thread
2–4 cm
UK, 1982

117 Wing-Wave 3
     Combination
        neckpiece
     David Watkins
     Neoprene over
        steel/wood
     20 cm d
     UK, 1983

118 Mt Hagen Hoopla
     Neckpiece
     David Watkins
     Neoprene over
        steel/wood
     20 cm d
     UK, 1981

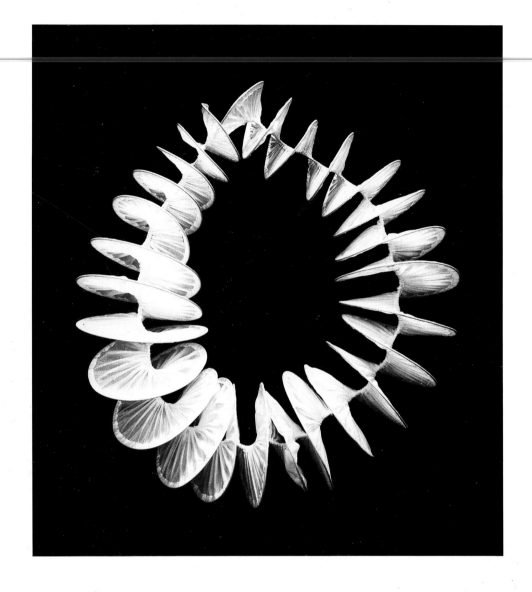

119 Necklace
    Jean-Paul Aleman
    Coiled wire covered
        in stitched silk
    30 cm
    France, 1982

120 Neckpiece
    Paul Derrez
    PVC, steel
    40 cm
    Holland, 1982

Overleaf
121 Neckpiece and
        two bracelets
    David Poston
    Titanium, forged
    14 cm, 6 cm
    UK, 1983

JEWELRY AS IMAGE

Mainstream
Figurative Work

Toothbrush and Paste. Brooch. John Plenderleith. Silver. 9.5 cm. UK, 1974

JEWELRY AS IMAGE
Mainstream Figurative Work

Translated into jewelry, bizarre fantasies may provide entertaining ornament. Of course, with abstract work, the observer and wearer can dance along with the maker through the choreography of form and harmony, but a direct appeal to the imagination is a necessary and attractive alternative. When confronted with something like Ralph Turner's international collection of plastic figurative jewelry, we have something to get to grips with immediately. Similarly, looking at Richard Mawdsley's brilliant but outrageous Gothic constructions, the viewer is immediately engaged in the question, 'What does it mean?'

Most of the objects in Fancy Goods (Ralph Turner's collection) are not especially bizarre or fantastic because they are only miniatures in plastic of humble day-to-day objects (such as breakfast cereal packets or hairdryers), with a leavening of images from the popular cinema (such as Tarzan). Nevertheless, many people are attracted by things in miniature – toy houses, model villages and, it appears, replicas of tins of baked beans as brooches. They all encourage good-humoured interest.

Laurie Taylor, an English sociologist, has written interestingly about Fancy Goods, although wisely he warns that writing about 'junk' jewelry can degenerate into 'junk' philosophy. He observed that the objects are a little downmarket of their wearer. And Taylor is right. Anyone with the slightest interest in the art and design world knows that etiquette about taste is as complicated as any other kind of social etiquette. You might, for example, genuinely like a concrete 'Cupid' ornament for your garden. If so, you risk being branded as tasteless, or downmarket, or *nouveau riche*. On the other hand, if everything else in your garden is well-thought-out and well designed, if your garden furniture is the design equivalent of the Mies van der Rohe *Barcelona* chair, you could have your concrete Cupid as a joke. Its presence would really let your friends know that you can distinguish good from bad, and more – that your tastes are so superior that having a little bad around the place simply cannot taint them. In fact, in some hands, with some people, the cleverness of the Fancy Goods style of jewelry could be stifling in its one-upmanship.

> Why do so many people love to wear such little jokes? [asks Taylor]. I think there are two main reasons. One . . . the desire to distance oneself from conventional jewelry which is redolent of security and a fixed life style; . . . The other, I believe, is the desire to call attention to oneself without striking too

pronounced a position. The little joke on the lapel or round the neck proclaims a mild sense of distance from conventional images but not a surrealistic subversion of everyday objects. It is something which tickles reality but leaves it undisturbed.

Tickling reality is a pleasant image but, if we are to believe Taylor, there is more to Fancy Goods than that. He commented: 'the miniaturised representations of commercial products are small insults to the real gods of our contemporary culture'. Not such a pretentious remark, perhaps. After all, it would be a brave young salesman who dared mock his company by wearing a comic version of it on his lapel.

Fancy Goods work is fun, it can be charming and its success is no surprise at all; Richard Mawdsley is quite different. Mawdsley's work is not coy, often it is not immediately attractive. Reactions tend first to be surprise, followed by praise for the skilled workmanship. The famous Feast Bracelet impresses people because on the table there are intricately formed, well-turned miniature bottles, jugs, flagons, fruit and cutlery. Miniaturization is fascinating and in this case all the more so because the objects have a degree of verisimilitude which almost suggests that they have been used, that they are 'real' and not 'toys'.

However, as Janet Koplos, in her excellent *American Craft* article on Mawdsley brings out, he has doubts about the Feast Bracelet. He knows it is a technical masterpiece, but is it anything more? Is it aesthetically sound?

Mawdsley raises a difficult point for himself. Why should it be anything more than a virtuoso demonstration of his technical skills? What ambitions ought a jeweler to have for such a piece of work? After all, it is difficult (although not impossible) to imagine succeeding in making an aesthetic or spiritual *tour de force*, a *Last Supper*, say, to be worn on the wrist – it would be subverted by its built-in dinkiness in the same way that Hollywood biblical epics are subverted by the belief that verisimilitude is just a matter of getting all the details correct. The Feast Bracelet is really all right because it is a complicated, involved object without any specific allusions; it does not prompt the viewer into inappropriate inferences about 'meaning'. Koplos correctly points out that the bracelet is saved from dinkiness by the colour of the silver. Had it been coloured, naturalistically, it would have been unbearable: a Fancy Goods epic. As it is, if your taste favours such objects, then you will see it as a well-designed, extraordinarily well-made ornament.

One barrier to appreciating Mawdsley's work is not of his making. There is an abundance of figurative ornament on sale in department stores and gift shops: some is cast in metal, some in resin and some in porcelain. Most of this work is attempting to be 'lifelike' or 'detailed' and it is frequently nostalgic or backward-looking. Most of it is second rate. Arguably, however, it is precisely because there is so much of this 'junk' around that there is no danger of Mawdsley and other comparable figurative jewelers suffering from total critical disdain.

Goneril, Regan, Cordelia, Belt buckle.
Richard Mawdsley. Silver, lapis lazuli.
8 × 3 cm. USA, 1976–77

Some of Mawdsley's work is less literal than the Feast Bracelet. A piece such as the Medusa   156
pendant is 'interpretative' and works well enough as an image of the woman-beast whose hair is
composed of writhing snakes. Everything about the Medusa's torso echoes the horrible notion
of the snakes, not literally, but obliquely through its machine-like aspect. The piece appears to
be weak only at one point: the expression on the figure's face is not so much alarming as vaguely
fraught and middle-aged. Yet, this is a pendant for wearing and therefore not an occasion for the
completely grotesque. And it is arguable that such a caveat – in this instance, limiting the
grotesque – underlines once again one of the limitations of jewelry: each time it strays towards
sculpture the question, 'Dare anyone wear this?', is pressing.

The Goneril, Regan, Cordelia buckle is a particularly successful Mawdsley work; it is involved,
interesting and elaborate, a combination which works formally in terms of design and
composition, and intrigues imaginatively because of its imagery. We might puzzle about the
title. Why call it Goneril, Regan, Cordelia? If it is necessary to have literary allusions, why do the
three figures look like triplets? In King Lear the three women behave in different ways and look
physically different. In fact, it ought not to matter what literary labels are given to work of this
kind. Its potential for 'meaning' is not bound up with literature but in its more general appeal to
the modern Gothic imagination.

Occasionally, jewelry is used to make direct social or political comment – a point which is
developed further in respect of the Canadian David Didur, as well as Otto Künzli, in the next
chapter. Here we show several examples by the American jeweler, Ron Ho, including his
pendant Clockwork Cohn – a clear, rather simple, comment on the nature of modern,   158
industrialized work. The pendant illustrates what Gary Griffin referred to as the American
jeweler's concern with using his or her philosophy about life as the basis for jewelry (p.15). Ho's

piece asks the question whether it is desirable to spend one's time at the behest of machines in order to earn a living; at the end of one's working life, the price paid in time might be too great, the rewards too meagre. This particular work might thus be described as a minor *memento mori*.

Clockwork Cohn is not wholly typical of Ho's work which, as the illustrations show, tends to be concatenations of objects with no direct story. They are ornate assemblages. Ho has travelled extensively throughout the Far East – Japan, Indonesia, Thailand – as well as in India and Nepal. 'These travels exposed me to the ornate patterns of the oriental cultures which had a deep influence on my work and brought me back to my original heritage of being Chinese.' Ho's artefacts, the animals especially, are finely observed, sometimes stylized and grouped *en masse* to create a dense, ornate effect.

Another American jeweler producing figurative work is Bruce Metcalf, mentioned in the preceding chapter as an example of expressionism in new jewelry. Metcalf is one of the very few modern jeweler-sculptors whose work has sufficient substance to withstand translation from pin or pendant to table sculpture. His works also have wit – not that they provoke belly laughs, rather a kind or wryness; they are odd objects. Most of the pieces have several common ingredients, such as the sensation of movement and the implied notion that something is happening and that we have caught the action midway.

In the two pins called Unprotected Moon and Protected Moon the action is all bound up with defence and attack. By making the mechanical or manmade objects, such as the daggers, appear semi-organic and sentient, Metcalf makes the piece ambiguous but tongue-in-cheek. There are no specific meanings in Metcalf's work and 'sculptures' such as the 'Moons' pins are maddening if you are trying to crack open the visual metaphor; there is no point in trying. It is doubtful if even Metcalf himself can say convincingly what the works 'mean', because these are objects with their own life. What retains a viewer's interest is the fact that the work has just enough realistic content in it to catch the imagination. It is a quite different category of figurative work to Ron Ho's Clockwork Cohn, with its nailed-down meaning, or to the Betsy King nostalgic brooch.

The scale at which Metcalf's jewelry and sculpture works is important. Some of the table sculptures are fifty centimetres high, but the idea of making the same kind of images very much larger would be appalling. The peculiar objects Metcalf has created would look ridiculous if they were enlarged to metre-size or more. Part of the interest of all miniature work is that we peer into, and not up at, the maker's imagination.

One of the difficulties facing the figurative jeweller, as we noted in discussing the work of Richard Mawdsley, is the ever-present threat of 'dinkiness'. In one sense, making art in miniature is much easier than making it big because any flaws in composition, shape and form are not as noticeable as when they are scaled up. And what looks charming at the scale of a few centimetres is boring when enlarged – a fact that rather too many painters of stripy abstract canvases overlooked in the early 1970s. Yet there remains the 'trinket factor' – that sense of trivia which derives from the truth that at the very small scale there is no room for gesture or action. One of Metcalf's successes lies in the way in which he creates 'room' in his pieces.

Another jeweler who, like Metcalf, has avoided the trap of dinkiness is Manfred Bischoff. His work is attracting attention not least because he has come up with some new shapes and ideas for ornament. Bischoff has raided the heavyweight territories of fine art and come back with Greek pillars and an energetic bundle of linework from the Picasso-Matisse school of rapid drawing. By rights this 'plagiarism' ought to have meant failure, but these stolen goods have been made into something very much his own. By breaking the pillars, daubing them, making an assemblage of them, and by taking the Picasso-Matisse line and mangling it into a calligraphy of his own, Bischoff has produced new ornament. The wire portrait brooch, irrespective of its being a brooch, shows some adept modelling; it is a good piece of 'drawing'. The materials he uses, such as styrofoam and wire, are light and comfortable to wear, though wearability has not, it seems, played much part in the design of the work. It does not 'relate' to the body – very little figurative work does.

However, the Israeli jeweler, Esther Knobel, whose warriors and sportsmen have won an enthusiastic following in Europe, insists that all her pieces are intended to work on the wearer, that they are incomplete without the wearer. She has explained that she is interested in the

Object. Avner Axelrod. Plastic, cloth. 20 cm.
Israel, 1982

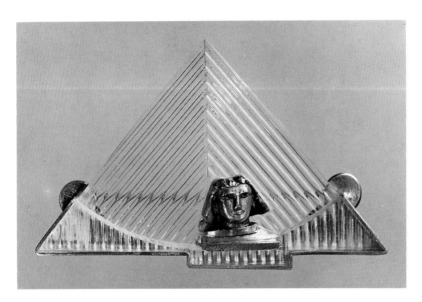

Brooch. Ulrike Bahrs. Gold, acrylic.
6 cm. West Germany, 1981

processes of jewelry-making, but makes no sketches or plans and has no idea at the outset how a finished piece will look. Tin cans are flattened into sheets out of which shapes are cut, and sometimes the pieces are embossed. The decoration of the warriors, with its reference to or association with camouflage, derives partly from some earlier work which for her was bound in with events relating to the wars between Israel and its neighbours. Realistically, however, Esther Knobel makes no claim that there is any 'political' content or metaphor for the wearer or observer of her work. For them the work is obviously decorative and playful.

Another Israeli, Avner Axelrod, has tried to make 'politics' into jewelry by producing 'medals'. Like Bruce Metcalf's work, that produced by Axelrod veers between wearable ornament and sculpture. Axelrod alludes to medals and uniforms through colour and the arrangement of shapes, but on second glance the dominant imagery is seen to consist of white mice, flowers and games redolent of childhood. Visually, these are interesting rather than pretty assemblages, but the 'meaning', their symbolism, is too esoteric.

Meaning and content in figurative jewelry usually breaks down into a straightforward division between the very literal, such as Ron Ho's Clockwork Cohn or Mawdsley's Feast Bracelet or Fancy Goods, and the open-ended ambiguities of Bruce Metcalf or Ulrike Bahrs, which let your imagination draw its own inferences. Figurative work goes adrift when the work is both ambiguous and yet intended to represent a narrow and specific range of ideas. Jewelers, like sculptors, sometimes have over-optimistic expectations that people will make the correct deductions about the specific meaning of their work.

119

The work of the Italian jeweler and sculptor, Bruno Martinazzi, might not seem to present any problems over interpretation and understanding, for it reproduces parts of the body. Yet these p.19 pieces are not, says Martinazzi, without meaning. The finger and hand pieces are intended to 142–3 remind us of the 'hand as a creative instrument of knowledge and invention, and meant to establish a relationship with others'. And in his rings the concept of measurement is important because it is 'a means of understanding the universe of which man is a part'. It is important to note that Martinazzi's ambitions as sculptor have always taken on the large, humanitarian themes which may be too big for most jewelers to contemplate. Again, there is a question of scale, of needing space to construct a substantial coherent metaphor – a space not usually provided by jewelry.

What all the best figurative jewelers are trying to avoid in their work, regardless of meaning, is cuteness. Cuteness bedevils jewelry in the same way that quick, slick, graphic tricks bedevil drawing. But in jewelry what can save a piece from banality is sheer quality of workmanship and the decorator's eye for good pattern – an excellent example from Britain is Sophie Chell's 125 brooch. In some respects, however, the figurative jeweler puts his or her neck on the block more boldly than the abstractionist. With figurative work there are fewer opportunities for getting away with arbitrary decisions – there are too many ways in for the observer or wearer to pick up points and criticize. The lay critic can pick up on 'poor' modelling or composition in a way that is harder with abstract work simply because the 'ground rules' are less obvious.

Although it is unwise to prophesy, it none the less seems likely that the next few years will see more and more figurative work of innovation and interest, partly because the abstractionists are coming to a logical, albeit temporary, conclusion in their ideas about the forms jewelry can take.

Opposite 122 Pins. Esther Knobel.
Painted tin. 15 cm. Israel, 1983

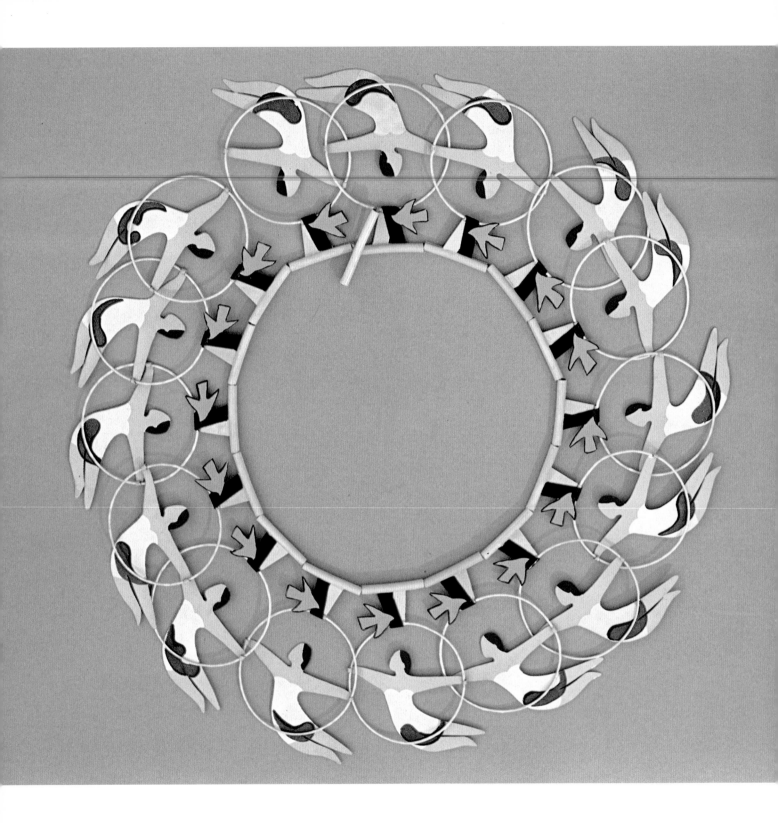

123 Necklace
Esther Knobel
Painted tin
25 cm
Israel, 1982

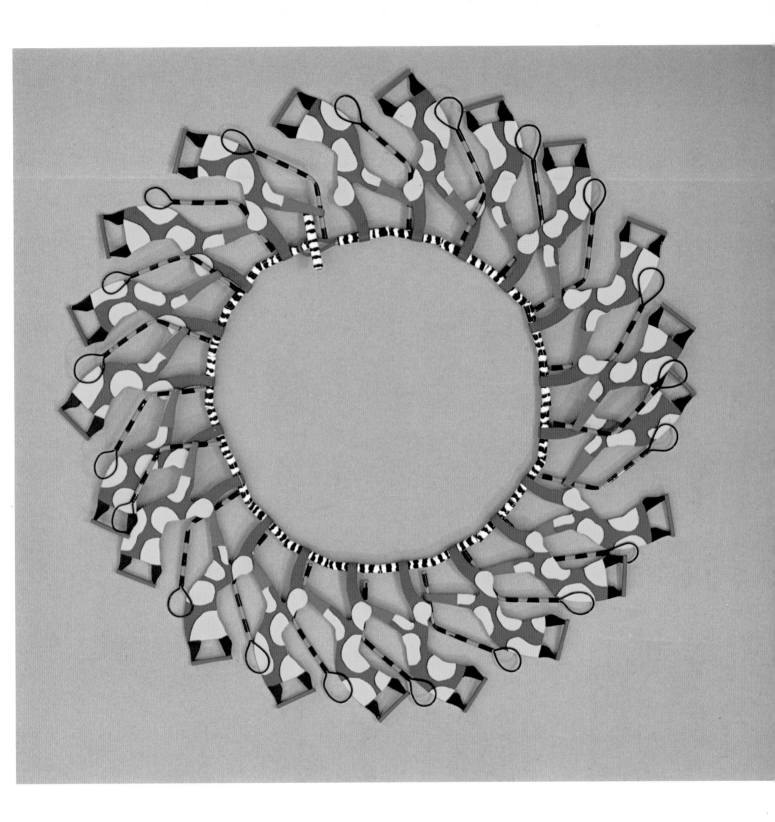

124 Necklace
     Esther Knobel
     Painted tin
     25 cm
     Israel, 1982

125 Pin
     Sophie Chell
     Anodized silver, gold
     6 cm
     UK, 1980

126–129
     Brooches
     From Ralph Turner's
          Fancy Goods Collection
     Plastics, resins, wood
     8 cm (largest)
     Australia, UK, USA, 1974–78

130 Pendants
William Harper
Gold, silver, enamel, pearl
7 cm
USA, 1980

131 Feast Bracelet
Richard Mawdsley
Silver, pearls, fabricated
11.5 cm
USA, 1974

132 Rose
   Gijs Bakker
   Colour photograph
     in laminated plastic
   60 cm
   Holland, 1983

133 Chrysanthemum
   Gijs Bakker
   Chrysanthemum leaves
     in laminated plastic
   30 cm
   Holland, 1983

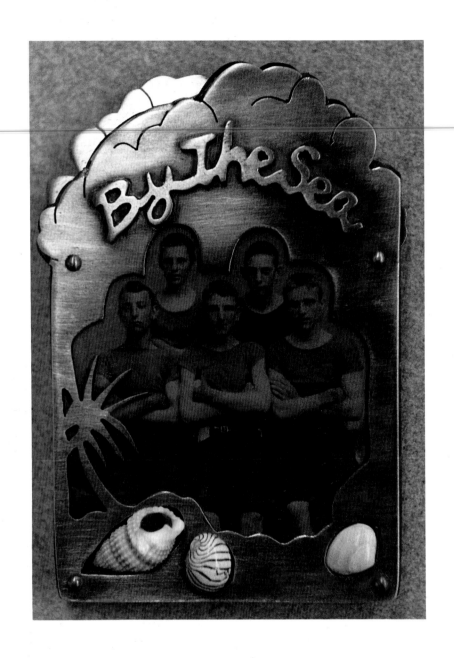

134 By The Sea
Pin
Betsy King
Silver, shells, tin,
plexiglass
7.5 × 5 cm
USA, 1977

135 Pin
Esther Knobel
Painted tin
15 cm
Israel, 1983

136 Treasures of the Orient
  Pendant
  Ron Ho
  Forged, fabricated
    silver, ivory,
    carved Chinese
    jade button
  22 × 9 cm
  USA, 1979

137 Bracelet
  E.R. Nele
  Gold, diamond
  7 cm
  West Germany, 1983

138 Gertrude's Bullish
    on America
  Necklace
  Ron Ho
  Fabricated silver with
    carved bullocks
    from India, beads,
    mother-of-pearl
  25 × 10 cm
  USA, 1981

139 Unprotected moon
   Protected moon
   Pins
   Bruce Metcalf
   Silver, brass, acrylic
   11 cm h
   USA, 1981

140 Only Partly of This World
   Object
   Bruce Metcalf
   Silver, brass, acrylic, plastic
   20 × 12 × 3 cm
   USA, 1980

141 Pliers pursuing a prickly figure
   Brooch
   Bruce Metcalf
   Silver, brass, acrylic, plastic
   10 cm h
   USA, 1982

142 Energy
   Rings
   Bruno Martinazzi
   Gold
   2 cm
   Italy, 1980

143 Venus
   Brooch
   Bruno Martinazzi
   Gold
   6 cm
   Italy, 1980

144–147
Four pins
Manfred Bischoff
Styrofoam, wire
15 cm
West Germany, 1981–83

148 Brooch
Gisela Seibert-Philippen
Gold, ruby
7 cm
West Germany, 1977

149 Brooch
   Ulrike Bahrs
   Gold, steel,
      screenprint on
      tinplate
   5 cm
   West Germany, 1980

150 Pin
   Manfred Bischoff
   Wire
   15 cm h
   West Germany, 1983

151 Oz East?
   Pin
   Julie Shaw
   Cardboard, felt,
      aluminum
   8 cm h
   USA, 1980

152 Bracelet, pin
   Ruudt Peters
   Acrylic, wire
   20 cm
   Holland, 1983

153 Brooch
   Hubertus von Skal
   Gold, steel, enamel
   5 cm
   West Germany, 1972

154 Into the Heart
   Pendant
   Ulrike Bahrs
   Gold, silver, acrylic
   6 cm d
   West Germany, 1979

155 Three rings
   Hubertus von Skal
   Gold, agates
   2 cm
   West Germany, 1972

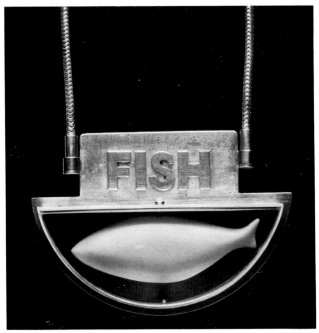

156 Medusa
   Pendant
   Richard Mawdsley
   Silver, lapis lazuli
   Fabricated, repoussé head
   20 cm l
   USA, 1982

157 Pendant
   Catherine Mannheim
   Silver, gold, ivory
   5 cm
   UK, c. 1978

158 Clockwork Cohn
     Pendant
     Ron Ho
     Silver, bronze cast toy,
        eye glass lens, watch cogs
     22.5 × 10 cm
     USA, 1977

159 Pin
     Glen Bodnar, Dan Donovan
     Pencil, plastic paint brush,
        white metal, copper
     15 cm l
     USA, 1982

Overleaf
160 Brooches
     Gary Wright
     Silver
     5 cm, 1.5 cm, 6 cm
     UK, 1976

JEWELRY AS THEATRE

Radical Departures

Crouching figure. Ladder neckpiece. Julia Manheim. Wire, plastic tube. 1.6 m, 1.3 m. UK, 1983

JEWELRY AS THEATRE
Radical Departures

'It's unthinkable for a man to turn up at work wearing an earring . . .', says Horton. Horton, career diplomat, is a character in Paul Theroux's *The London Embassy*, which contains a long, witty passage dealing with the appropriateness (or not) of wearing jewelry. Horton is almost physically sick at the sight of his otherwise 'A1' communications officer wearing a single ring through his ear, but the man delegated to tell the officer that the earring has to be removed observes: 'I was surprised to find it a lovely earring. . . . It was the sort of detail that makes some paintings remarkable; it gave his face position and focus – an undeniable beauty. It was the size, and it had the charm, of Shakespeare's raffish earring in the painting in the National Portrait Gallery.' Nevertheless, the ring eventually goes, though it would spoil a good story to say how.

We all know that jewelry, like anything else a person chooses to wear, tells us about that person's taste and personality. But jewelry is rarely used by jewelers to make comment about the conventions and taboos surrounding either the making or the wearing of it. However, one man who has had a success in doing just that is the Swiss-born Otto Künzli, one of the most intelligent makers in the jewelry world and also one of the most sceptical.

The frequent play that Künzli makes with geometric shapes, with the block, cube and stick, has outraged jewelers and critics alike. They have responded by thinking that such activity is tomfoolery and childish, that anyone can do it; in any case, they ask, who would wear this work? Who indeed? The first point is that cube-and-block jewelry is not seriously intended as commercial ornament but as a reflection on jewelry and the limited conventions within which it works. Künzli makes us reflect on the narrowness, at any given point in history, of what society finds acceptable in dress. And the interest is not simply in reminding us that the conventions exist, but in highlighting the fact that they are arbitrary – that what is permissible changes.

Now it might be objected that this is all rather trivial. We know about fashion, but what Künzli demonstrates, or at any rate, what hostility to his work indicates, is how seriously people fight and argue when these otherwise 'arbitrary' conventions are broken. Künzli's subject matter deals in part with what we might term the 'Horton principle' – the unthinkable in body decoration. Some of Künzli's reflections, such as his Wall brooch, are taken to absurd extremes, but other examples of his work are better mannered in their flouting of the rules. For example, if you re-read the Paul Theroux account of the man wearing the earring, and then apply it to the

164

Stick, cube, block pins. Otto Künzli. Wood grain wallpaper, hardfoam. Stick 35 × 2.5 × 0.5 cm. Cube 5 × 5 × 5 cm. Block 17 × 10 × 2.5 cm. West Germany, 1983

173 portrait shown in this chapter of the man wearing Künzli's House brooch, you will recognize an aptness in the description. The Künzli brooch might be said to give the face 'position' and to be the very detail that completes the portrait – and yet, by other criteria, it is absurd. The brooch is worn with a beautiful seriousness, and a dignity, which almost but not quite renders the object perfectly normal – it is the fine balance of the 'normal' with the 'unconventional' in this portrait that it gives it an edge.

There is a point about Künzli's work which needs clarifying. In producing his unconventional objects, he is not saying that they are, in fact, perfectly reasonable, obvious things to wear (although, in a different time or culture they *could* be). You do not demonstrate your great enlightenment and understanding of all things modern and liberal by rushing off in one of Künzli's creations. To do so is to miss the point. The point is to draw attention to the existence of conventions as real and binding, albeit at the same time temporary and arbitrary.

Künzli loathes the power and status that so much conventional jewelry parades through its use of precious materials. Consequently, he has devised a range of ornaments which is functional, pretty, cheap and, as far as possible, dissociated from money. These are the brooches 165–8 and pins he has produced in every conceivable geometric form, each with gaily decorated surfaces. Yet, even this work raises questions. If you look at the portraits of the two women – the one in a yellow sweater, the other a purple dress – it is probable that you will find their Künzli brooches perfectly acceptable ornament. You may or may not like the work, but these women, both of whom have the good fortune to be young and pretty, are perceived as being able to 'carry the work off'. But look then at the man wearing the (admittedly more elaborate) Künzli tie-pin. What is basically ornament, no different in kind to that worn by the women, appears radical and unconventional – a violation of the Horton principle. These pictures do more than draw attention to convention; they underline the reality of it by providing a demonstration which we can see for ourselves of what is acceptable and unacceptable in everyday life.

With work of this kind, adjectives such as 'witty' and 'humorous' are often scattered around with abandon but without much evidence. As an example of Künzli's wit, we offer the man   168
wearing the floral, decorated brick. This brick upstages a number of male-dominated conventions, from the vaguely lecherous (or, alternatively, very formal) flower in the buttonhole, to the politician's rosette. It is an example of well-mannered rudeness. In *A Map of the World*, a play by the British writer David Hare, a young man gets very annoyed with a middle-aged man, who has been polite but rude to him. Then he explodes: 'You're like all those people who think that if you say "Excuse me" at one end of a sentence and "Thank you" at the other, you are entitled to be as rude as you like in between.' In between the politeness of his object and that of his models, Künzli is being quite rude.

Künzli's work, like most of that shown in this section, is at its most effective in photographs where the maker has complete control over all aspects and the wearer and the object are fixed into a single, photograph-jewelry event. The extent to which the photograph and art gallery dominate radical work can be seen simply by looking through the pictures here. This is also true of Marjorie Schick's huge neckpieces, which are clearly unwearable in the day-to-day sense of the term. Her large works are ritualistic, ceremonial, with more than a nod in the direction of tribal dress and tribal dance.

There is a tendency among critics to debunk the sort of work produced by Schick as being flash-in-the-pan – a quickly worked-out idea with no particular development behind it – but that is not the case. Schick, who trained first as a metalsmith, began in 1967 to make large papier-mâché bracelets. Papier-mâché enabled her to work large whilst keeping the weight under control, and it also provided her with a surface to paint. Later she abstracted both line and colour from these works and gradually evolved her current compositions.

Schick has pushed the components of twentieth-century abstract art to its proper decorative   198
conclusion. Yet, whilst this makes her work a decorative art, it does not make it jewelry; it has become an abstract art with its roots in jewelry. This obvious, but important, distinction saves us from a world of nonsense. At the moment, some 'artist'-jewelers are unnecessarily confusing themselves – and others – by insisting that their work is jewelry despite the fact that it cannot be worn except, possibly, under very limited circumstances.

Left, Armpiece. Marjorie Schick. Papier-mâché. 12 × 18 cm. USA, 1969

Above, Pins. James Evans. Lint, cotton. Canada, 1983

185, 196   Pierre Degen is the most controversial 'craftsman' to have shown under the auspices of craft or decorative art in either London or New York. His recent work has consisted of performance-based pieces or 'sculptural' works and has involved all manner of large objects, including large ladders and huge black balloons on sticks. It is possible that certain critics understand, or at least articulate, Degen's ideas more clearly than Degen himself. Certainly there was a sigh of relief, mixed with enlightenment, when *Crafts* magazine published its review of Degen's London exhibition (September 1982). The review was written by one of Britain's younger and most important poets, Christopher Reid. In order to appreciate Reid's analysis fully – and perhaps to note also a degree of poetic sympathy – it is useful to know that he is one of the 'Martian' poets – a school of influential British writers taking their name from a poem entitled 'A Martian Sends a Postcard Home' (by Craig Raine). This is a poem in which the familiar world is seen through the eyes of an alien. And so, to quote from Reid:

> Degen has told me how he delights in the appearance of ordinary objects – brooms, garden implements, a window-cleaner's apparatus – but not so much for the way they have been made, as for the spectacle they provide in their workaday context. A number of things he likes are being shown in his exhibition, alongside pieces made by him. The point is that one is enabled to see these otherwise normally neglected artefacts with greater vividness in the ironic light that Degen's work casts upon them. I can say from my own experience that, after watching their maker trying on this piece and that in the setting of his studio, it was possible to step into the outside world and feel a surge of innocent

Large loop. Pierre Degen. Fiberglass, string.
160 cm d. UK, 1982

amazement at the great radiant sail-like contraption that we have learned to call an umbrella . . . or any of the other mysterious properties with which the inhabitants of our civilisation have chosen to extend or encumber themselves.

Undoubtedly such an interpretation is reasonable; it is also coherent. Degen's work has taken upon itself the wider category of speculation and interpretation associated with the fine arts, with sculpture in particular. And it is interesting that to do this Degen has had to work on the large scale; it confirms the view expressed earlier that one of the limits which keeps jewelry to an essentially decorative function is its literal lack of physical space in which to create gesture and to develop metaphor. Degen has had to sacrifice practical wearability (an essential characteristic of jewelry's definition) in order to make, comment and explore ideas about the sorts of things we wear or carry. The work once had some roots in jewelry, but recently has had to be taken outside jewelry in order to comment and reflect upon it.

Less controversial is Susanna Heron, whose development Ralph Turner has explained in his historical review. She was one of Britain's most important modern jewelers, although now she is developing as a sculptor. Her work, which has explored geometry and colour in wearable ornament, progressed to 'wearables' with a kinship to clothing but, by 1983, it was clearly to be looked at and not worn. If it was ornament at all, it was ornament for a room. Nevertheless, her wearables have given us some beautiful examples of decorative art, not least the blue and red 'hat' illustrated here. 171–2

150

161 Susanna Heron and, most importantly, Caroline Broadhead have been dominant among the radical jewelers in Britain, but Broadhead's recent radical (as opposed to her mainstream) offerings have tended towards clothing. Her 'veil' or 'headpiece', which we illustrate, is clearly an extreme work in the sense that it is seen at its best, and can be worn only at its best, on a model in a gallery or posing for a photograph. Nevertheless, the same piece, because of its flexibility, can be worn more practically by collapsing it into different, more convenient shapes, as a 'ruff' around the neck or pulled down across the shoulders.

What marks the different futures for the two makers is the likelihood that Caroline Broadhead's work will remain wearable. Susanna Heron, on the other hand, became interested in the grouping of objects and the scope that these groupings then provide for sculptural metaphor. These objects may, or may not, continue to take with them the references to the body.

Whatever the precise 'content' of work by people such as Heron or Degen, it is generally oblique and metaphorical. As we have seen, very few jewelers attempt direct socio-political comment in their work. This is not surprising. Apart from the fact that very few makers see jewelry as an appropriate medium for such comment, it is also the case that many of them, with Otto Künzli a notable exception, are rather insular. Ideas and issues beyond the world of the decorative arts do not inspire their work. It can thus come as a considerable surprise when an overt political comment is attempted in the context of a jewelry exhibition. David Didur, the

162 Canadian jeweler, produced a 'necklace' and pendant called Medal for Dishonour for the exhibition *Jewelry In Transition*. The work was made of live and dead matchsticks, firecrackers and thread, and the pendant was in the shape of the United States of America. Didur listed his materials more radically: Political Firecrackers, Industrial Iron (pendant), Strike Anywhere

Cigarette Performance Pack. Tom Saddington. Steel.
180 cm. UK, 1980

151

Matches, Short Fuse, and Threads of Credibility. Here was an anti-cruise missile protest, conceived on the premise that you never know when it (or a cruise missile) is likely to blow up. It was shrewd of Didur to make the piece for an exhibition likely to attract publicity but, of course, its success was dependent upon its rarity; if every jeweler started making protest jewelry then its impact would disappear, unless it was widely worn.

The political imagination is also at work in the recent examples produced by West-German jeweler Wilhelm Mattar. Mattar's work is a mixture of the abstract and the figurative, but it has about it a hint of brutality which is surprising and mildly discomforting in jewelry. The 'earpieces' 192–5 are placed in the arms of toy soldiers to become banners or weapons, and, as the portrait photographs show, when worn they can be given a degree of menace. Here we see jewelry played up as a symbol of machismo, while usually it is purely ornamental. With the implied violence, there are also, perhaps, sexual connotations, although it is too easy with this sort of work to begin manufacturing metaphors and associations – like pulling an endless string of flags from the conjurer's hat. Mattar's work presents an upmarket, radical chic version of Punk, which has taken various forms since it began as a late-1970s fashion among adolescents who wore razor blades, nails and safety pins to establish a version of tribal identity for themselves and to distance themselves from adult authority.

Graham Hughes, editor of the London magazine *Arts Review*, was quite right when he said that the most effective parallel between radical jewelry and other art forms was the theatre. Hughes, however, intended the parallel to be a criticism. He said (*American Craft*, September 1983): 'On stage, the audience can enjoy the fun and beauty and fantasy and visual philosophy of all sorts of strange gear but can't appreciate them with the full senses, for the simple reason that the footlights are in between. Stage props don't look too good in real life because you get too close to them, and you start analyzing them with those senses which the theater designer puts out of reach: touch, weight, texture, even smell.' He concluded that such work is really a statement for the stage, not real life. This criticism would be sound had the makers he was criticizing (Degen, Heron, Broadhead and others) maintained that their radical work was simply wearable ornament. In fact, most of the work pictured in this section is exploring ideas, much as the theatre is used for exploring ideas. As such it offers, as the theatre offers, a number of possibilities for criticism, debate, acceptance or rejection, with the knowledge that, in the end, the audience, the purchaser and the wearer always decide.

Opposite 161 Neckpiece, veil. Caroline Broadhead.
Nylon monofilament. 45 cm, 25 cm d. UK, 1983

162 Medal for Dishonour
Neckpiece
David Didur
Firecrackers, iron, matches, cotton
27 × 21 cm
Canada, 1983

163 Necklace
Stirling Clark
Pasta
37 cm
UK, 1983

164–168
Brooches
Otto Künzli
Wallpaper, hardfoam
Top left, 43 × 20 × 5 cm

Top right, 13.5 × 12 × 5 cm
Bottom left, 23 × 11 × 2 cm
Bottom right, 19 × 14 × 1.5 cm
Opposite, 13 × 9 × 6 cm
West Germany, 1983

169 Ladder neckpiece
   Julia Manheim
   Plastic tube
   120 cm
   UK, 1983

170 Paper neckpiece
   David Watkins
   Paper spiral
   20 cm
   UK, 1983

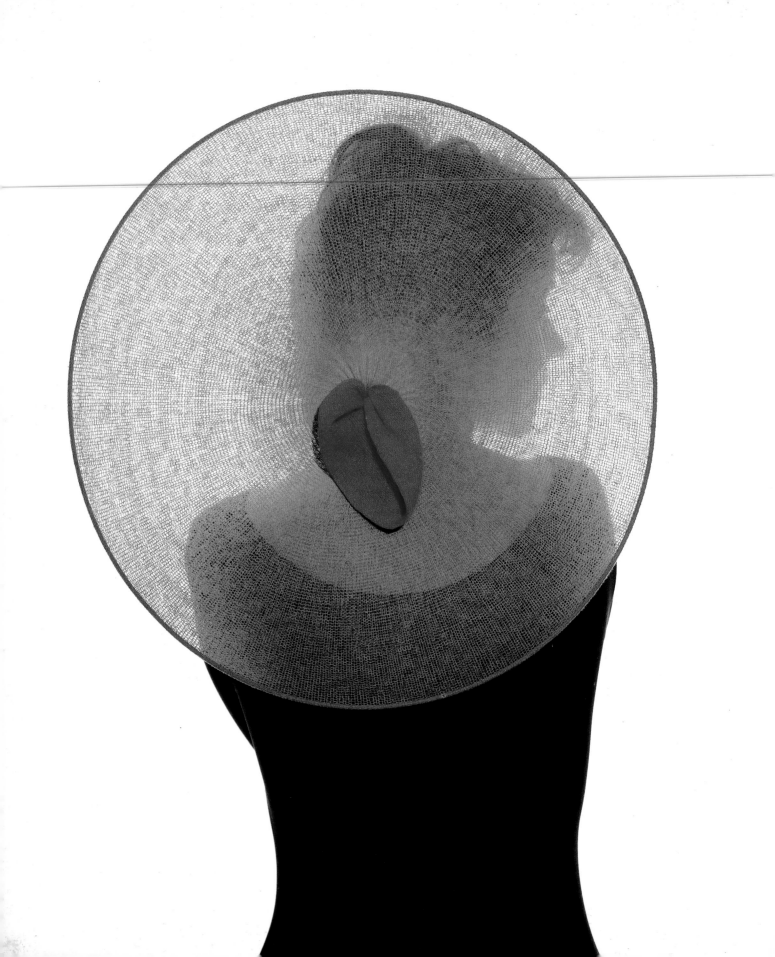

171 Wearable
Susanna Heron
Cotton on wire frame
46 cm d
UK, 1982

172 Wearable and non-wearable objects
Susanna Heron
Painted papier-mâché, cotton, nylon,
wire
Largest wallpiece, 60 × 10 cm
Largest wearable, 62 × 22 cm
UK, 1981–82

173 House
Brooch
Otto Künzli
Paper, hardfoam
8 × 6 × 7 cm
West Germany, 1983

174–177
Earpieces
Gerd Rothmann
Silver
2.5 cm
West Germany, 1983

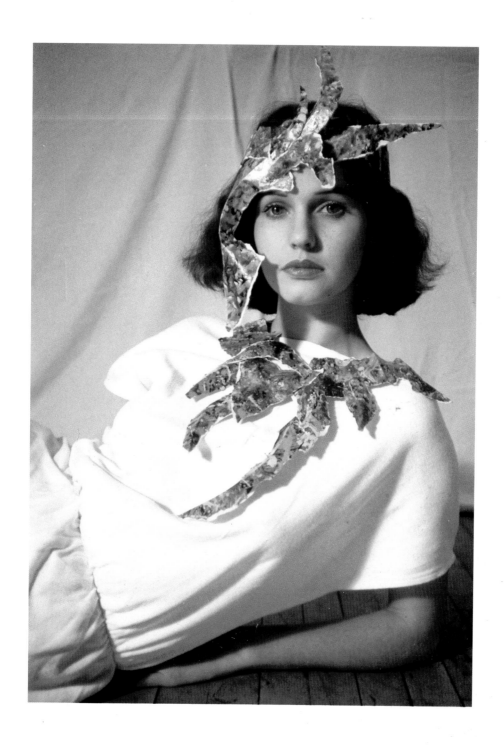

178 Shoulder and body piece
   Lam de Wolf
   Shredded fabric
   120 cm
   Holland

179 Head-, neckpieces
   Michael Petry
   Paper and paint
   28 cm
   USA, 1983

180 These Shoes Are
       Made for Walking
    Performance-based
       jewelry
    Michael Petry
    Paint, paper
    6–15 cm
    USA, UK, 1983

181 Shirt with
       seven sleeves
    Caroline Broadhead
    Silk
    2.5 m
    UK, 1983

182 Shirt with
       seven necks
    Caroline Broadhead
    Cotton
    2.5 m
    UK, 1983

183 Neckpiece
    Susan Sanders

184 Party Jewelry
   Richard Karpyshin
   Eight framed life-size
      photographs, red
      enamelled crosses
   8 cm
   Canada, 1983

185 Personal environment
   Pierre Degen
   Wood, string
   140 × 140 cm square
   UK, 1982

186 Ready Made
   Catalogue cover
   Exhibition at
     Galerie Mattar
   Cologne, 1981

187 Pendant
   Lutz-Albrecht Quambusch
   Lacquered bones, leather,
     pheasant feathers
   23 cm
   West Germany, 1982

188 Head jewelry
   Barbara Heinrich
   Polished steel, aluminum
   30 cm
   West Germany, 1981

189 Printing set
   Wendy Ramshaw
   Brass stamps, ink
   2 cm
   UK, 1982

190 Neckpiece, armpiece
   Kai Chan
   Dogwood, thread
   22 cm, 10 cm
   Canada, 1983

191 Jeans piece
   Jan Wehrens
   Blue steel
   16 × 10.6 cm
   West Germany, 1982

192 Blue Point
   Earpieces
   Wilhelm Mattar
   Aluminum, silver, steel
   9 cm
   West Germany, 1982

193 Earpieces
   Wilhelm Mattar
   Gold, steel
   7 cm
   West Germany, 1982

194, 195
German-Japanese Friendship
Earpieces
Wilhelm Mattar
Gold, steel
13 cm
West Germany, 1982

196 Ladder piece and
     balloon
    Pierre Degen
    Rubber, wood
    2 m, 60 cm d
    UK, 1983

197 Ladder piece
    Julia Manheim
    Plastic tubing
    60 cm
    UK, 1983

198 Neckpiece
    Marjorie Schick
    Painted wood
    60 cm h
    USA, 1983

Overleaf
199 Primary Orbits
    Neckpiece
    David Watkins
    Neoprene over steel
    39 cm d
    UK, 1983

4

JEWELRY AND DISSENT

Recent Directions

Monte-Zum-A-Black face and My-An-Dynasty-Silver face. Brooches. Andrew Logan. Glass, resin and pearls. 150 cm. UK, 1992

JEWELRY AND DISSENT
Recent Directions

Jewelry is a shrewd monitor, reflecting the ups and downs not only of money and fashion, but also of political, social and cultural change. The preceding chapter dealt with the most radical spirit in jewelry's history, the seeds of which were sown in times of affluence. This chapter summarizes a far less confident decade, with retrenchment and hard-headed financial control governing our lives and ruthlessly pruning the arts. Politically, it could hardly have been a more turbulent period.

This cutback in the expansionist spirit of the arts was not a clean amputation for jewelers, but a slow, steady drift towards a more orthodox approach. Some countries fared better than others, but Europe – and particularly Britain with its long-drawn-out recession – saw several designers adopt a more commercial attitude. With the ingredients changed, the diet was now sometimes more conservative than before; there was more figurative and narrative work overrun with nostalgia and more 'classic' modern styles.

Yet, despite this downward curve, experiments in jewelry continued. Good, forward-looking work was made. With its definition broadened, jewelry had achieved a new art status which attracted young people who saw that a creative career could be eked out of jewelry making. Role models had established that jewelry could be a vehicle for change by using new ideas and alternative materials. Young designers applied this to suit their own abilities and to face the practicalities of a harsher financial climate.

Only a handful of jewelers make a living from one-off designs; most produce work in small quantities with time set aside for unique, more expensive pieces. Jane Adam, Daphne Krinos, Mah Rana and Catherine Hills are four young British designers who have met with some success by using this formula. Geoff Roberts is another. His training as a printmaker and sculptor show up brazenly in his jewelry. Its brilliant colours and lively images stand out from the more well-mannered understatements peculiar to some British work. Despite his lighthearted approach there is very little sense of whimsy in Roberts' work, particularly his large theatrical pieces: best suited perhaps for those who are larger than life.

Roberts' love of burlesque is also at the heart of another well-established British jeweler and sculptor, Andrew Logan. As instigator of the Alternative Miss World contest, Logan became famous, welcoming competitors of all sexes and ages with spectacular and often ambiguous

221

results. His jewelry is equally bizarre, transforming the wearer with glittering metropolitan glamour. Wolfgang Liesglen (self-styled, Wolli the Kid) from Germany, Peter Tully from Sydney and Kate Durham from Melbourne are others who enjoy excess in their jewelry repertoire.

220   A taste for excess also surrounds the pithy work of Peter Chang, a Londoner who now lives in Glasgow. The use of colour in his synthetic fantasies is loud; in fact it screams at you. His forms are exotic and weird, exposing jewelry's intrinsic quality: sensuality. This is jewelry at its most seductive and Chang squeezes every succulent drop from the unlikely materials.

Some other British jewelers manage to produce fresh interesting work that leaves more orthodox design in the doldrums, despite the current pressures to conform. Thomas Eisl's logical solutions to jewelry provide aesthetically challenging work. Rubber tubes and inflated balloons form part of the functioning locking systems to brooches, bracelets and the like. Hans Stofer's jewelry and objects are equally unorthodox, with collections that include 'fruit bowl' constructions which enclose one grape, one apple, etc. Louisa Hunter is also hugely inventive,

214   with a ravenous appetite for found objects that she builds into punchy jewelry. Jared Taylor drew inspiration for his use of plastics from his walks around the disused docks in his home town, Dundee. With plastic sheet and resins, he transformed the massive, unwearable metal images he saw into light, warm, tactile jewelry of considerable character.

Surviving as an artist in times of recession is far from easy, though in Scandinavia the Government helps by supporting not only young artists but also those who have already made significant strides with their work. Few Scandinavians could have contributed more to their

212   country's reputation over the last 20 years than Tone Vigeland from Norway. Vigeland adapts reductivist principles of unit construction into refined body ornament, which is yet not ornamental. Despite the lengthy construction process, there is never a sense of overwork or heavy confrontation with technique. Although it has an affinity with modern sculpture, Vigeland does not follow trends in contemporary art in her work, unlike some designers who are obsessed with the latest 'isms' coined by the world's curators. Olli Tamminen, a strong and silent Finn, is also steadfast to his Northern roots, finding sufficient nutrition there to feed his creativity, making jewelry that is tranquil, timeless and of special beauty.

There has been during the past few decades an explosion of cultural influences criss-crossing the globe, energizing jewelry with fresh and sometimes exotic input. Jung-Hoo Kim (Korea), Mah Rana and Maria Wong (UK) and Kai Chang (Canada) are good examples of this fertilization. With

226   some, however, a sense of cultural identity is harder to trace in their work. Roger Hutchinson was born in Trinidad before leaving for Australia, where he worked for a while as a graphic designer. In the late 1970s he studied jewelry under Ragner Hansen, a Scandinavian-born goldsmith now living in Tasmania. Hutchinson's cool, sensitive work carries the hallmarks of both these influences with little evidence of his Caribbean background. His choice of aluminum

allows him to experiment without compromising his ideas or scale. As the material is not expensive, it makes his modernist work accessible to a wider public.

The Dutch provide us with their own democratic solutions on how to survive as a jewelry designer without compromising ideas too much. In Holland, multiples and small, signed editions have long been an effective means of bringing good jewelry design to the public; Maria Hees, Johanna Hess-Dahm and Joke Brakman have used these methods since the 1970s. More recently, Stephan Seyffert's stagey ring collections and Nel Linssen's sensuous paper collars 208 have followed these principles, as has Herman Hermsen, whose editions took the rise out of jewelry and the diamond industry with a dazzling cynical collection of synthetic gems.

Younger reformers in Europe now have different objectives that expose their own undiluted interpretations of jewelry. Bernard Jongstra and Johanna Titselaar (self-styled, Gem Kingdom) from Holland celebrate jewelry's erotic, fetishistic qualities. Lucy Sarneel, also from Holland, 201 uses transference of symbolism and images of status in her work. Simon Fraser in London explores the content of body adornment and social issues with performances and events, and Wolf von Waldow in Hamburg creates jewelry for those with coyish genitals. Despite these deviations, mainstream jewelry flourishes, as Amsterdam's Galerie Ra — with its stock of affordable, innovative jewelry from around the world — well illustrates.

Although the Dutch excel in providing us with jewelry that we can afford, they are not alone in this egalitarian activity. In Germany, even some master goldsmiths feel compelled to open up their order books to a more general public. Hermann Jünger, no less, brought out a pristine 225 edition of boxed jewels in 1987: rock crystals, semi-precious stones and gold-plated units that could be worn selectively on thin platinum or gold wire. Jünger's prices were reasonable enough to bring his beautiful work within the reach of many more people. George Dobler is another German jeweler who supplements his one-off pieces with a well-thought-out group of limited editions. The main body of his work, however, deals with the aesthetics of materials that are often unadorned and natural, opposing organic forms with rigid metal structures.

Goldsmithing in Germany is prolific and presents us with some exciting young talent. Alexandra Bahlmann centres her work on the time-consuming and arduous process of chain-making. She has an impressive repertoire of strong interlocking shapes affirming her confident approach to design. Karl Fritsch and Detlef Thomas appear to share a love of expressive 210 ornament. Fritsch builds towers of glistening crystal for rings that are out to impress. In a quieter mood, his linear finger rings are more modest and effective. Thomas's jewelry mixes design metaphors that span the centuries, yet it is acutely contemporary. In the late 1980s his pendants of gold and silver, built as skeleton constructions like Tatlin's tower or space laboratories, were impressive. More recently, his work reveals a rich organic flavour in which there are Baroque tendencies. He is a jeweler to watch.

Pendants. Olli Tamminen. Soapstone, ebony, silver, brass. 150 cm (largest). Finland, 1993
Chain. Alexandra Bahlmann. Oxidized silver. 50 cm. Germany, 1990

Halle is a large industrial district and the powerhouse of former East Germany. The town lies between Weimar and Dessau, homes of the most celebrated art school of modern times – the Bauhaus. The Hochschule für Kunst und Design (High School for Art and Design) in Halle is also an important centre for art education, where Yvonne Galley and Andrea Wippermann graduated in 1985 and 1987, respectively. With powerful sculptural jewelry, Galley asserts her style with an armoured, almost brutal, spirit of medievalism. Wippermann is equally forceful and at her most confident with silverware, though the term is perhaps too bourgeois for her provocative work. With blatant irreverence for the precious metal they use, the work of both these young artists has a raw, red-blooded beauty; a homage to a pre-industrial age. However, jewelers in other countries have lost themselves in eclectic rummaging of pre-industrial art. This is true of America and Australia where some have found rich pickings scavenging American Indian and Aboriginal cultures. Generally, this culling has not thrown up much interesting work, being mostly simplistic and misunderstood adaptations from the original source.

209 The Introduction of the first edition predicted that the Australian Carlier Makigawa was a young jeweler worth watching. Ten years later she is now recognized internationally for her papier-mâché and steel jewelry, with its affinity to architectural design. Her best work illustrates the designer's dictum, 'keep things simple'. Susan Cohen and David Walker are two more Australian jewelers who follow this discipline: Cohen with bracelets of cool, perforated aluminum and Walker with brooches of steel grids, bedded into cushions of deep copper.

Resilience is a fundamental quality of goldsmiths in Israel; their success could not have been harder won. Jerusalem's Bezalel Academy was founded by some members of the Bauhaus who escaped the Holocaust. Esther Knobel studied and taught there, and her influence can be seen in the quality and inventiveness of the work of her former students, such as Vered Kaminski, Einat Primo and Kobi Roth, from Tel Aviv, who is a good example of Knobel's nurturing. His   218 strong work is charged with powerful images, some of conflict and menace.

Independent galleries play a crucial part in the creative developments of jewelry. Louise Smit   200 Gallery in Amsterdam is a strong alternative to Gallery Ra, with a policy which could not be more different. Simply put, Louise Smit caters for a richer palette, with gold being the chief ingredient. Its policy is nothing if not discerning, with impressive exhibitions by some of the world's leading goldsmiths: Giampaolo Babetto, Manfred Bischoff, Peter Skubic, Falko Marx and   204,206 Robert Smit. Smit is an interesting figure in the art-jewelry world. In the late 1960s and early 1970s he provided, as did Marion Herbst, an alternative view to those reductivist attitudes exposed by Bakker and Van Leersum. Smit was not opposed to embellishment and used colourful acrylics and computer programming in his work. But, in the late 1970s, he abandoned jewelry altogether for drawing, returning again to his jewelry bench in the mid-1980s to cause ructions. The implications of this were far-reaching and are worth looking at more closely.

With a flamboyant collection of large-scale gold jewelry, Smit demonstrated that the use of precious metal need not be *de rigueur* for the modern jeweler in Holland. In the Stedelijk Museum's *Concerning Amsterdam* exhibition in 1986, Smit's work caused something of a rumpus, as volumes of gold re-emerged centre-stage in the Dutch capital. Accusations were made by jewelry designers that he was re-establishing jewelry as a class symbol for a privileged elite. 'Old fashioned "schmuck" which re-instates the jewel as a status symbol and an object for investment' was how Gijs Bakker judged Smit's work. Other vehement arguments against so blatant a use of gold were aimed at Smit. Smit lamented the passing of the Dutch jewelers' individual approach to aesthetics, which he claimed had been replaced by dogma and ideas handed down from the fine arts. He defended his right to use gold and unleashed his love of the metal with alloys of rare colour which he composed himself.

Now Gijs Bakker, once the champion of democracy in Dutch jewelry, also uses gold and diamonds in his work. I asked him the reason for this change of attitude. 'Society and politics change and the world is a different place now. When Emmy [van Leersum] and I were young there was far less equality. Nowadays most of us are more or less equal – at least in Holland. The message we gave out with our radical forms and new materials was done with conviction almost 30 years ago; it made its impact then and so we moved on with society.' Time may have had a mellowing effect on Gijs Bakker, but it has not blunted his wry humour. His jewelry today is still loaded with irony and symbolism and those diamonds are mostly set in PVC. These   207 developments and the return by artists to precious metals are not restricted to Holland, but the Dutch example well illustrates jewelry's facility to monitor social change.

We discussed in the previous chapter Otto Künzli's sceptical approach to jewelry and his unease with the use of gold. But, in 1985 he composed an extraordinary gold necklace that was unwearable. The piece was not unorthodox in its design, in fact it could hardly not have been more simple. 'Chain' was exhibited in Künzli's solo exhibition *Of Symbols and Other Things* at the Art Gallery and Museum, Kelvingrove, Glasgow in 1992. Virginia Rigney, the Assistant Keeper, explains the story behind the making of the piece.

'Chain' is composed of 48 wedding rings which date from 1891 to 1981. To obtain them Künzli placed a series of advertisements in the Munich daily newspaper saying simply 'I collect wedding rings'. It gave a 'phone number, and for one year he became so obsessed with the gathering that he found he could work on nothing else. Some rings arrived in the post, accompanied by notes such as 'Otto – ring for your chain. The engraving is KM (Crete) to PV (Olympia) – two Greeks who wed in New York. Also enclosed is a blue bead to keep away the evil eye when you cut the band'. With others he visited the owners and recorded the stories they told in a diary . . . 'The father-in-law fell in Stalingrad in the fall of 1942, the ring was returned many years later by a comrade' – or 'A ring 8kt not engraved from her first husband' – her comment 'He was a brutal dog'. Künzli had taken the responsibility for these rings from their owners by cutting them to form the chain. However, despite its formal beauty who could bear the weight of these individual histories by placing it around their neck?'

The use of precious metals by many artist jewelers is now widespread. Manfred Bischoff's Styrofoam and wire work features in the chapter dealing with figurative jewelry. The contributions there are largely celebratory and fun; but not so Bischoff's, which portray symbols of destruction: broken pillars, flame and mangled calligraphy, etc. Ten years or so later his style and materials have changed, though – despite some animated offerings – his gold faceless figures, clutching empty vessels, are contemplative and melancholic.

The soul-searching, ethical debate in the 1970s and 1980s concerning jewelers' role in society was not universal. In Italy Francesco Pavan, Arnaldo Pomodoro and Bruno Martinazzi never wavered from using gold. This was also true of Gerda Flöckinger, Wendy Ramshaw and Breon O'Casey in the UK and Philip Sajet in Holland. Giampaolo Babetto from Padua continues his distinguished career as a goldsmith, interpreting cool, Late Modernism in jewelry of breathtaking beauty. Post-Modernism also saw its style widely interpreted in gold, though with far less aplomb than in Daniel Kruger's pendants of the late 1980s. This small collection depicted fragments of architectural details which added to his already wide repertoire.

It is exceedingly difficult to sustain a creative career with fresh, intelligent ideas that build consistently into an artist's repertoire. Two German jewelers, Elisabeth Holder and Rudolf Bott, are impressive in this respect. During the past decade, Holder's work has grown in stature, with strong sculptural solutions to jewelry that nevertheless keep within the parameters of function.

Bott develops his impressive serpentine forms in large-scale sculpture and jewelry, both of which retain a warmth and strength with tensions similar to work of the artist, Eduardo Chillida.

Falko Marx, the German goldsmith, has a way with the most mundane materials: iron, ink, tin   206 cans or common tap water, framed in gold, all focus our attention on jewelry of subliminal quality. Robert Ebendorf, a pioneer in modern jewelry in the USA, also explores a wide range of everyday materials in his work. Both these men are meticulous craftsmen, juxtaposing fragments of found objects with precious metals. They are, however, not merely recycling scavenged materials, but refashioning them to reaffirm their aesthetic values.

Helen Drutt and her gallery in Philadelphia is a tireless advocate of the applied arts – a term, I suspect, she would be unlikely to use. Several of her gallery artists from both sides of the Atlantic are illustrated in this chapter, including the fantastic creations of Overstreet and Kranitzky.

Much American jewelry of this genre is a vehicle for the artist's agenda, where strong imagery and narrative express personal ideas and opinions. It is also the principal difference between European and American work, which over the years has had a polarizing effect. Fred Woell's and Richard Mawdsley's works are good examples of this provocative use of jewelry. The narrative approach is also the platform for the intelligent work of Bruce Metcalf. We have looked at his work earlier, but he continues to be an important figure in American jewelry, though he is far from happy with the state of the art. He writes: 'My pins also indirectly address the state of contemporary jewelry, which I believe is oriented mostly toward very safe conceptions of good design and good taste. I find very little to think about in most American jewelry, which disturbs me. After all, the human body is probably the most intimate and subversive arena for artworks.' If one supports the idea that jewelry should be used as propaganda, then one can understand Metcalf's point of view. This philosophy, with its own criteria, was – and still is – unique to North America; the work, though charged with coded messages, usually does not travel well.

As Metcalf has suggested, there are a growing number of American jewelers who have opted for a cooler design ethic, closer perhaps to the European model, replacing the racy narrative work with more reductivist designs. ROY and Boris Bally, Jo Wood and Daniel Jocz are positive   208,211,227 examples of this. But narrative jewelry represents American immoderation in full flood and I would hate to see its polemical spirit snuffed out by mere blandness. The energy and guts of some work should be celebrated as part of the vast range of American culture, with all its rhetorical character.

Whatever the issues, materials or categories, jewelry is a social communicator, for good and for bad. The work of the 1970s and 1980s had fundamentally widened the field and if what followed was less assured, the old traditions had been challenged. There was no going back.

Opposite 200 Koningin Bello (Queen Bello). Brooch. Robert Smit.
Gold, pearls, paint. 23 cm. Holland, 1992

201 Craft Guild
   Chain
   Lucy Sarneel
   Gold, silver, steel, wood, thread
   22 cm
   Holland, 1993

202 Rings
   Cynthia Cousens
   Silver, gold
   3 cm
   UK, 1993

203 Headpiece
   Adele Tipler
   Electroformed gold-plated copper
   22 cm
   UK, 1993

204 Creator
     Brooch
     Manfred Bischoff
     Gold, coral
     11 cm
     Germany, 1992

205 Auf Ewig Dein
     Brooch
     Norman Weber
     Granite, silver
     9.5 cm
     Germany, 1992

206 Brooch
     Falko Marx
     Gold, water, gold leaf
     9.5 cm
     Germany, 1989

207 Waterman
     Brooch
     Gijs Bakker
     Laminated photograph by Bruce Weber
     PVC, diamonds
     12 cm
     Holland, 1991

208 Necklace
     Nel Linssen
     Reinforced paper
     18 cm
     Holland, 1992

209 Brooch
     Carlier Makigawa
     Monel, silver
     10 cm
     Australia, 1991

210 Pendants
     Detlef Thomas
     Gold, silver, rock crystal
     9.5 cm
     Germany, 1987/89

211 Brooches
     Joe Wood
     Patinated silver, gold
     7.5 cm
     USA, 1990

212 Neckpiece
     Tone Vigeland
     Patinated silver
     31.5 cm
     Norway, 1989

213 Ring
     Philip Sajet
     Patinated silver, rose quartz
     4.5 cm
     Holland, 1993

214 Necklace and handpiece
     Jared Taylor
     Polyester resin, acrylic paint,
        polystyrene
     30 cm, 10 cm
     UK, 1991

215 Dandling
   Brooch
   Kim Overstreet
      and Robin Kranitzky
   Micarta, plexiglas, copper, silver,
      postcard fragments, found objects
   7.5 cm
   USA, 1990

216 A penny for your Feelings
   Brooch
   Fred Woell
   Silver, brass, copper
   7 cm
   USA, 1991

217 Curler
   Pendant
   Gordon Stewart
   Silver, anodized aluminum
   7.5 cm
   UK, 1993

218 Bugs
   Brooches
   Kobi Roth
   Aluminum, safety pins, blades,
      fishing hooks, ready made
   8 cm
   Israel, 1990

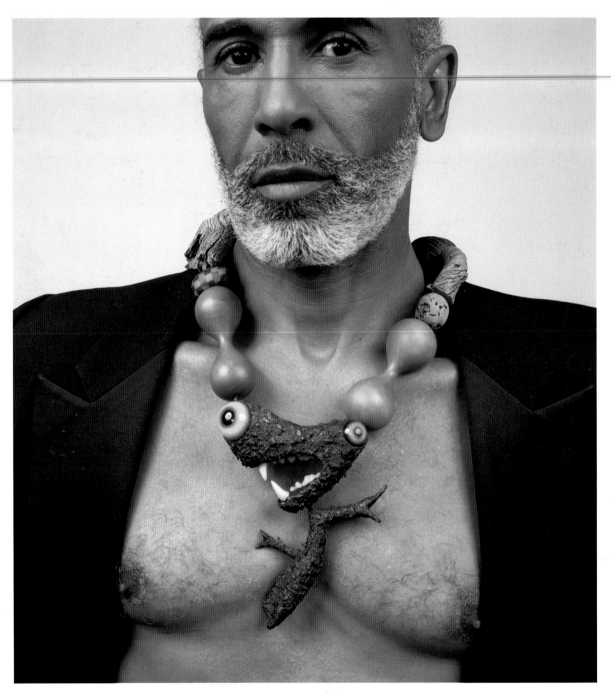

219 Wood neckpiece 7
Bruce Metcalf
Maple, cherry, oak, walnut, pine,
    rosewood, cork, glass eye,
    tagua nut, plastic teeth,
    brass, cord, gold leaf, pigments
35.5 cm
USA, 1992

220 Bracelet
   Peter Chang
   Laminated mosaic
      and thermo-formed acrylic,
      PVC, polyester resin
   15 cm
   UK, 1993

221 Quiver of Fish
   Neckpiece
   Geoff Roberts
   Printed acrylic and oxidized steel
   25 cm
   UK, 1993

222 Rings, brooches and hair-grip,
      composed of found objects.
      'Finds' catalogued as personal diary.
   Louisa Hunter
   Plastic, rubber, steel
   10.5 cm (largest)
   UK, 1991/93

223 Ring and earrings
     Rudolf Bott
     Gold
     5 cm
     Germany, 1993

224 Rings
     Elisabeth Holder
     Zinc, silver
     3.0 × 1.5 cm
     Germany, 1990

225 Boxed necklace with
        nine interchangeable units
     Hermann Jünger
     Gold-plated silver and
        bronze, rock crystal,
        haematite, gold wire
     14 cm
     Germany, 1990

226 Armrings
     Roger Hutchinson
     Anodized aluminum, neoprene
     13 cm
     Australia, 1992

227 Ring
     Daniel Jocz
     Nickel-silver, polymer clay
       with pigment
     6 cm
     USA, 1992

228 American Dream
     Bracelet
     ROY
     Recycled STOP sign, silver,
       diamonds, ruby
     15 cm
     USA, 1993

BIOGRAPHIES OF MAKERS

Aleman, Jean-Paul b. France 1954. Self-taught textile designer. Exhibitions include *Jewelry Redefined*, London 1982.

Babetto, Giampaolo b. Italy 1947. Studied at the Instituto d'Arte, Padua; Academia di belle arti, Venice. Important exhibitions include Stedelijk Museum, Amsterdam 1977; Van Reekummuseum, Apeldoorn 1978; Tokyo Jewelry Triennale 1983. Solo exhibitions: Galerie Cada, Munich 1987; Louise Smit Gallery, Amsterdam 1990.

Bahlmann, Alexandra b. Germany 1961. Studied at the Gerrit Rietveld Akademie, Amsterdam: Akademie der Bildenden Künste, Munich (under Hermann Jünger). She specializes in chains and necklaces; her fastening systems are often an integral part of the aesthetic. Selected exhibitions: Louise Smit Gallery, Amsterdam; Galerie Spectrum, Munich; *Constructions in Jewelry and Metal Objects*, Oriel Gallery, Cardiff; *Ornamenta 1*, Schmuckmuseum, Pforzheim; *Internationale Schmuckszene '90*, Handwerksmesse, Munich; Jugend Gestaltet Prize and Herbert-Hoffmann Prize, Munich.

Bakker, Gijs b. Holland 1942. Studied at the Instituut voor Kunstnijuerheidsonderwijs, Amsterdam. He has had a number of significant solo or two-person jewelry exhibitions with his wife, Emmy van Leersum. These two makers, both very influential, were especially important in the late 1960s and early 1970s. An early major joint exhibition was *Sculpture to Wear*, Amsterdam 1966 and London 1967. Bakker now works mainly, but not exclusively, as an industrial designer and among his design exhibitions *The Industrial Art of Gijs Bakker* (Crafts Council, London 1978) was important. Retrospective: Centraalmuseum, Utrecht 1989. *Holes Projet*, Galerie Ra, Amsterdam 1993.

Bally, Boris b. USA 1961. Studied at the Carnegie Mellon University, Pittsburgh; apprenticed to Alexander Schaffer, Basel, Switzerland. Refined and stylish ornament combining grid, metal constructions with wrapped fibrous coverings. Selected exhibitions: *Studio Production, More than One*, American Crafts Museum, New York; *Internationale Schmuckszene '93*, Handwerksmesse, Munich. Solo exhibitions: Morrison-Rink Precious Metals Gallery, Portland, Oregon.

Bauer, Frank b. Germany 1942. Studied gold- and silversmithing, then design and architecture in Hamburg. His design and architectural interests are important influences on his jewelry – indeed, he also works in applied design. Currently living and working in Australia.

Becker, Friedrich b. Germany 1922. Studied at the Werkunstschule, Düsseldorf. Becker is respected for his excellent workmanship and his innovations with kinetic jewelry. He is an influential teacher and his own work is in most of the important European collections, such as the Worshipful Company of Goldsmiths, London, and the Schmuckmuseum, Pforzheim.

Bennett, James b. USA 1948. Studied in the department of Gold- and Silversmithing at State University College, New Paltz, New York. Has been apprenticed to Barry Merritt (goldsmith) and assistant to William Harper (enamellist). Now one of the USA's leading modern enamellists. Important group exhibitions include *Good As Gold*, Washington D.C. 1981 and USA tour.

Bischoff, Manfred b. Germany 1947. Studied Fachhochschule, Pforzheim (under Reinhold Reiling, 1922–83); Akademie der Bildenden Künste, Munich. Selected solo exhibitions: Helen Drutt Gallery, Philadelphia; Louise Smit Gallery, Amsterdam; Museum Het Kruithuis, s'-Hertogenbosch. Selected mixed exhibitions: *Contemporary Jewelry* touring exhibition, Institute for Foreign Cultural Relations, Stuttgart; *Ornamenta 1*, Schmuckmuseum, Pforzheim; *Facet 1*, Kunsthal, Rotterdam.

Boekhoudt, Onno b. Holland 1944. Studied at the Vakschool Schoonhoven and the Kunst und Werkschule, Pforzheim. Teaches at the Gerrit Rietveld Akademie, Amsterdam. Important exhibitions include *Schmuck International 1900–1980*, Vienna 1980; Galerie Ra, Amsterdam 1977, 1979, 1981, 1983, 1991. Visiting Lecturer, Royal College of Art, London 1991–93.

Bott, Rudolf b. Germany 1956. Studied Goldschmiedelehre bei Hanau; Studium der Bildenden Künste, Munich. Work includes large-scale sculpture, silver and goldsmithing techniques, with inward-turning interlocking shapes of strength and character. Exhibitions include Galerie Rehklau, Nuremberg; Germanisches Nationalmuseum, Munich; Gallery Rezac, Chicago; Galerie Marzee, Nijmegen; Treykorn Galerie, Berlin. Public collections: Museum für Kunst und Gewerbe, Hamburg; Badisches Landesmuseum, Karlsruhe; Schmuckmuseum, Pforzheim; Dannerstiftung, Munich.

Brakman, Joke b. Holland 1946. Studied at the Gerrit Rietveld Akademie, Amsterdam. She is one of the leading 'reductivist' jewelers in Holland, placing great emphasis on the wearability of her work. Her jewelry has been widely exhibited and is in many public collections, including the Stedelijk Museum, Amsterdam.

Brink, Mecky van den b. Holland 1950. Studied textiles at the Gerrit Rietveld Akademie, Amsterdam. Developed her own textile jewelry in 1979 and, like several young designer-jewelers in Holland, has been impressed by the use of textiles and colour in the work of the English jeweler, Caroline Broadhead. Mecky van den Brink's work is in museum collections in Arnhem and Amsterdam, and in the University of Amsterdam.

Broadhead, Caroline b. UK 1950. Studied at the Central School of Art, London. Her early work involved colouring ivory but she became interested in less restrictive materials. By 1977 she was producing bound-cotton necklaces and in 1978 she devised an influential design whereby a wearer pushed his or her hand or head through tufts of nylon held in place in a wood or silver frame. She was one of the first of the new jewelers in Europe to use textiles and her use of bright colour can be seen as a continuation of the pioneering work of Fritz Maierhofer and Claus Bury. She has exhibited widely and is represented in several important collections, including the Knapp Collection, New York (*The Jewelry Project*). Retrospective: Crafts Council Gallery, London 1990. *On the Edge: art meets craft*, Crafts Council Gallery, London 1993.

Bury, Claus b. Germany 1946. Studied at Pforzheim as a goldsmith, but his major innovation was to combine gold and acrylics. In 1972 he shared the prize for the International Jewelry Competition at the Schmuckmuseum, Pforzheim. Following a highly successful contribution to a show at the Electrum Gallery, London (*Objects and Acrylic Jewelry*, 1972), Bury was invited to teach at the Royal College of Art, London. Later, at the Bezalel Academy of Art, Jerusalem, his work was experimental and sculptural. Although he was a major influence on modern jewelry throughout the 1970s, by the end of the decade he had decided to work solely as a sculptor — which he now does in the USA.

Cepka, Anton b. Czechoslovakia 1936. Studied in Bratislava and Prague and became a leading figure in modern jewelry in his country. He is a sculptor as well as a jeweler. For more examples of his work see the catalogue to *Schmuck International 1900–1980*, Vienna 1980. *Cepka and Novák*, Schmuckmuseum, Pforzheim 1988–89.

Chan, Kai b. Hong Kong 1940, Canadian citizen. Studied at Chung Chei College, Chinese University of Hong Kong; Ontario College of Art. He is an interior designer, but his contributions to jewelry have been shown in *Jewelry Redefined*, London 1982; *Jewelry In Transition*, Toronto 1983; *Art by Design*, Canada House, London 1984. Solo exhibition: Galerie Ra, Amsterdam 1989.

Chang, Peter b. UK 1944. Studied graphic design and sculpture at Liverpool College of Art; printmaking and sculpture at Slade School of Art, London. The influence of graphic design is reflected in his handling of colour, sometimes reminiscent of the psychedelic images of the 1960s. Recent exhibitions include solo shows at Galerie Ra, Amsterdam; Helen Drutt Gallery, Philadelphia; David Gill Gallery, London; Galerie Biro, Munich. Public collections include Aberdeen Art Gallery and Museum; Crafts Council Collection, London; Museum of Applied Arts, Helsinki; Kelvingrove Museum, Glasgow; Victoria and Albert Museum, London; Contemporary Arts Society, London.

Cohen, Susan b. Australia 1952. Trained as a graphic designer prior to studying jewelry and silversmithing at the Royal Melbourne Institute of Technology, Victoria. Work in the late 1980s was orientated towards product design: aluminum briefcases and bracelets of perforated metal made with precision. More recently Cogan's work has taken on a subversive character, with 'cosmetic manipulations' for the ageing face to help 'celebrate the lines of wisdom and experience'. Selected solo exhibitions: Melbourne City Art Gallery; Contemporary Jewelry Gallery, Sydney. Group/mixed exhibitions: *Australian Contemporary Arts*, Australian National Gallery, Canberra; *Internationale Schmuckszene '87*, Handwerksmesse, Munich; *The 20th Anniversary Show*, Electrum Gallery, London.

Cousens, Cynthia b. UK 1956. Studied Ipswich College of Art; Loughborough College of Art; Royal College of Art, London. Has established a reputation for discreet surface patterning and colouring of silver jewelry, often interpreting abstract forms from nature. Exhibitions include: *British Jewelry*, Crafts Council, London; *Internationale Schmuckszene '90*, Handwerksmesse, Munich. Solo exhibitions: Scottish Gallery, Edinburgh; Leeds City Art Gallery. Public collections: Worshipful Company of Goldsmiths, London; Crafts Council Collection, London.

Degen, Joël b. France 1941. Studied English at Montpelier University and did not become a jeweler until settling in the UK in 1965. He is a De Beers *Diamonds Today* prizewinner and is highly regarded as a craftsman, with work in several public collections including the Worshipful Company of Goldsmiths, London, and the National Gallery of Victoria, Australia. Not related to Pierre Degen. More recently, he took part in the *From Platinum to Paper* exhibition at the Leslêy Craze, Gallery, London.

Degen, Pierre b. Switzerland 1947. Studied jewelry at the Ecole d'Arts Appliqués, La Chaux-de-Fonds, Switzerland. Worked as a jewelry designer at Bucherer AG and as a technician in the jewelry department at the Central School of Art and Design, London; currently lecturer at Middlesex Polytechnic, London. He is regarded as one of the most radical of the new jewelers and his exhibition *Pierre Degen-New Work* (Crafts Council, London 1982) generated considerable argument. He has shown extensively throughout Europe. Awarded Françoise van den Bosch Award, Amsterdam 1985.

Derrez, Paul b. Holland 1950. Studied goldsmithing but became known for jewelry which used non-precious materials and which was designed to be worn either by men or women. In 1976 he founded the highly influential Galerie Ra in Amsterdam. A frequent juror for exhibitions, he has his own work in the collection of the Stedelijk

Museum, Amsterdam, and in the Cleveland Collection of Contemporary Jewelry, Middlesbrough.

Didur, David b. Canada 1953. Studied in New York, Florence and Tokyo, as well as at Nova Scotia College of Art and Design. He has exhibited mainly in Canada, including *Jewelry In Transition*, Toronto 1983.

Dobler, George b. Germany 1952. Studied goldsmithing in Pforzheim. Like Manfred Bischoff, George Dobler is unusual among younger German jewelers in his preference for non-precious materials and a generally lighter interpretation of his craft. He had a solo exhibition at Galerie Ra, Amsterdam 1981, 1990; group exhibitions include *The Jewelry Project*, London 1983, Perth International Crafts Triennial, Art Gallery of Western Australia, 1989.

Dziuba, Gabriele b. Germany 1951. Studied under Hermann Jünger, Munich. Important group exhibitions include *The Jewelry Project*, London 1983.

Ebendorf, Robert b. USA 1938. Studied at the University of Kansas. Professor of Art at the State University of New York. Work in public collections, including Schmuckmuseum, Pforzheim; Cooper-Hewitt Museum, New York; Twentieth Century Decorative Arts Collection, Metropolitan Museum of Art, New York. Contributor to many international exhibitions, including *Ornamenta 1*, Schmuckmuseum, Pforzheim 1989.

Eisl, Thomas b. Tyrol 1947. Lived in England since 1969. Currently Eisl explores logic and function, which are the mainstays of his idiosyncratic approach to making. His repertoire centres around highly imaginative designs for furniture, lighting and jewelry that are aesthetically challenging with a twist of humour. Eisl does not wish to catalogue the numerous exhibitions and public collections where his work has been and can be seen.

Evans, James b. Canada 1952. Studied at Nova Scotia College of Art and Design. Evans is one of the innovators in Canadian jewelry and potentially one of those likely to make a contribution to the new-jewelry movement of art-orientated work. He appears to take his cue from Europe rather than North America. Important exhibitions include *Jewelry In Transition*, Toronto 1983.

Fisch, Arline b. USA 1931. Studied at Skidmore College, New York; University of Illinois. She has had numerous solo exhibitions in the USA and UK, including Helen Drutt Gallery, Philadelphia; Electrum Gallery, London 1987. She is well known for pioneering a technique in which strands of silver are knitted together, sometimes creating a lace effect. She is the author of *Textile Techniques in Metal* (1975) and a noted teacher.

Fok, Nora b. Hong Kong 1953. Studied Hong Kong Polytechnic; Brighton College of Art, UK. Group exhibitions include *The Jewelry Project*, London 1983; *Jewelry Redefined*, London 1982.

Flöckinger, Gerda b. Austria 1927. Emigrated to England in 1938. Studied fine art at St Martin's School of Art, London;

jewelry and enamels at the Central School of Arts and Crafts, London. Established her own studio workshop in 1955 and between 1962 and 1968 lectured at Hornsey College of Art in London, where she formulated a course on modern jewelry. Flöckinger was a lone pioneer of alternative jewelry in Britain in the 1950s. With her undisputed talent and strength of character she was the first in the UK to build a career as an artist in jewelry. Her work has seen few radical changes over the years, but continues to reflect her consistent pursuit of refined ornament. She has exhibited internationally for more than four decades. Main solo exhibitions: British Crafts Centre (now Contemporary Applied Arts), London 1968; Victoria and Albert Museum, London 1971 and 1986. Public collections include Worshipful Company of Goldsmiths, London; Victoria and Albert Museum, London; Schmuckmuseum, Pforzheim; Crafts Council Collection, London. Awarded a CBE 1991.

Fraser, Simon b. UK 1960. Studied Sheffield City Polytechnic; Royal College of Art, London. Performance-based work and thematic collections. Events include: *Alchemy with a Piano*, 24-hour jewelry performance with Gillian Salmon and Peter Fountain: deconstruction of piano into jewelry for auction for London Lighthouse, AIDS Charity, ICA London; *Simon Fraser's One Night Stand*, Queen Elizabeth Hall, London; *A Catwalk Collection: Jewelry composed of dog biscuits*.

Fritsch, Karl b. Germany 1963. Studied at the Goldschmiedeschule in Pforzheim and the Akademie der Bildenden Künste in Munich, under Hermann Jünger and Otto Künzli. Inventive use of precious metals, gemstones and crystals using organic forms, sometimes with elaborations. Exhibitions include: *Ornamenta 1*, Schmuckmuseum, Pforzheim; Galerie Spectrum, Munich; Louise Smit Gallery, Amsterdam.

Galley, Yvonne b. Germany 1966. Studied at Burg Giebichenstein Hochschule für Kunst und Design (under Renate Heintze and Dorothea Prühl). Contributor *Schmuck Burg Giebichenstein 1970–1992*, Museum des Kunsthandwerks, Grassimuseum, Leipzig, 1993. 1st prize: DDR Schmuckwettbewerb.

Gem Kingdom

Jongstra, Bernard b. Holland 1960

Titsellar, Johanna b. Holland 1962

Bernard Jongstra is self-taught. Johanna Titselaar studied at Akademie voor Beeldende Kunsten, Arnhem. Idiosyncratic interpretations of jewelry with fetishistic overtones. Exhibitions: Galerie Intermezzo, Dordrecht; Gemeentemuseum, Arnhem; *Internationale Schmuckszene '92*, Handwerksmesse, Munich, *Facet 1*, Kunsthal, Rotterdam.

Grosse-Ruyken, Rita b. Germany 1948. Studied in Munich (under Hermann Jünger) and Paris. She sees her work both as jewelry and as sculpture and, unlike most applied artists, tries to incorporate metaphor in it. Exhibits widely in West Germany and is usually represented in international group shows.

Harper, William b. USA 1944. Studied at Western Reserve University, Cleveland. Exhibited throughout USA and also in Europe. His catholic tastes in applied arts are reflected in the eclectic references in his work to a wide range of exotic and tribal cultures. Harper's work is held in several American public collections, including the American Craft Museum, New York; Metropolitan Museum of Art, New York. Exhibitions include: *William Harper-Selected Works, 1978–91*, Frankin Perrasch Gallery, New York; *Facet 1*, Kunsthal, Rotterdam 1993.

Hees, Maria b. Holland 1948. Studied at the Akademie voor Beeldende Kunsten, Arnhem. In the mid-to-late 1970s she began to treat jewelry as part of her industrial design activity, using manufactured materials and industrial components. She worked closely with Maria Staajes – both were pupils of Gijs Bakker.

Herbst, Marion b. Germany 1944. Studied at the Gerrit Rietveld Akademie, Amsterdam. A founder member of the B.O.E. group (1973) and instrumental in showing young Dutch jewelers an alternative to the reductivist De Stijl aesthetic favoured in the early 1970s. Exhibited extensively in Holland, UK, Belgium. Solo exhibitions include Galerie Ra, 1981. Major retrospective at the Van Reekummuseum, Apeldoorn 1982. Work in public collections, including Stedelijk Museum, Amsterdam, where she was given a major retrospective of her work in 1993.

Hermsen, Herman b. Holland 1953. Studied at the Akademie voor Beeldende Kunsten, Arnhem. Important group exhibitions include *Views on Jewelry, 1965–1982*, Amsterdam 1982; *Some Dutch Jewelry*, Bristol 1984. Solo exhibitions: Galerie Ra, Amsterdam 1989; Galerie V & V, Vienna 1990.

Heron, Susanna b. UK 1949. Studied at the Central School of Art, London. First solo exhibition at Electrum Gallery, London 1972. A series of solo exhibitions since then have charted her development as a major influence in new jewelry in the UK and Holland. With her husband, photographer David Ward, she chose the works for *The Jewelry Project*, a collection of modern European jewelry (1980–83) for the New York collectors, Malcolm and Sue Knapp, first shown as an exhibition at the Crafts Council, London 1983. Her own work is in many public and private collections, including Crafts Council, London; Victoria and Albert Museum, London. Now working as a sculptor.

Hess-Dahm, Johanna b. Switzerland 1947. Studied goldsmithing in Zürich. Solo exhibitions include Galerie Ra, Amsterdam 1982, 1984; Galerie Spectrum, Munich 1986.

Hilbert, Therese b. Switzerland 1948. Studied in Zürich under Reinhold Reiling, and in Munich with Hermann Jünger. Has exhibited widely, including *The Jewelry Project*, London 1983. Perth International Crafts Triennial, Art Gallery of Western Australia. Solo exhibitions: Galerie für Modernen Schmuck, Frankfurt; Galerie Spectrum, Munich.

Ho, Ron b. Hawaii 1937. Studied Education at the Pacific Lutheran University; University of Washington. He has travelled extensively in South America, Europe and the Orient and many of his works are assemblages using objects found on his travels. Exhibited widely throughout the USA.

Holder, Elisabeth b. Germany 1950. Studied at the Staatliche Zeichenakademie, Hanau; Fachhochschule, Düsseldorf; Royal College of Art, London. Works in UK. She has lectured in Australia and her group exhibitions include *The Tenth Year*, Electrum Gallery, London 1981; *Tendenzen 1982*, Pforzheim; *Ring/Ringe*, at three locations in 1983: Aspects, London; Galerie Spectrum, Munich; Galerie Mattar, Cologne. Collections include Crafts Council, London; Schmuckmuseum, Pforzheim; Goldschmiedehaus, Hanau; Museum für Kunstgewerbe, Berlin. Recent exhibitions: *Influential Europeans*, Crafts Council Gallery, London 1992; solo: *Jeweler's Work*, Washington D.C., Electrum Gallery, London.

Holdsworth, Annie b. Australia 1953. Studied at the Royal Melbourne Institute of Technology. Like others in her generation she is finding a style separate from the all-pervasive West European influences. She has exhibited quite widely and her work is in most state collections in Australia.

Honing, Willem b. Holland 1955. Studied at the Gerrit Rietveld Akademie, Amsterdam. Exhibitions include Galerie Ra, Amsterdam 1982; *London-Amsterdam*, Crafts Council Gallery, London 1988; Perth International Crafts Triennial, Art Gallery of Western Australia 1989.

Hunter, Louisa b. UK 1969. Studied Cumbria College of Art & Design and Middlesex University under Caroline Broadhead and Pierre Degen. Hunter's jewelry is composed of found objects – often picked up in the street – such as lolly-pop sticks, drinking straws, buttons, plastic hair grips, etc. Each piece of jewelry is recorded in a personal diary giving the place and date of the find of each component. Her jewelry is represented in the Cleveland Contemporary Jewelry Collection, Middlesbrough.

Hutchinson, Roger b. Trinidad 1954. Emigrated to Australia in 1960. Worked in graphic design and studied gold and silversmithing under Ragnar Hansen at the Tasmanian College of Advanced Education. Hutchinson explores the lightweight properties of anodized aluminum to construct large-scale armpieces with designs that find parallels in modernist sculpture. Exhibitions include *Objects to Human Scale*, Crafts Council of Australia tour; *Indulgences*, Crafts Council Gallery, Sydney; *Internationale Schmuckszene '92*, Handwerksmesse, Munich. Public collections: Australian National Gallery, Canberra; Queen Victoria Museum and Art Gallery, Launceston; Art Gallery of South Australia, Adelaide.

Jocz, Daniel b. USA 1943. Studied Philadelphia College of Art; University of Massachusetts. Included in his wide repertoire are a collection of rings built of polymer clay in organic forms of brilliant colours. Selected exhibitions: Elaine Potter Gallery, San Francisco; *Jewelry USA*, SNAG, American Craft Museum; *Internationale Schmuckszene '92*, Handwerksmesse, Munich.

Jünger, Hermann b. Germany 1928. Studied at the Staatliche Zeichenakademie, Hanau. Former Professor of Goldsmithing at the Akademie der Bildenden Künste, Munich. Jünger's importance to modern jewelry is considerable and will become more so as his work becomes widely known in the rest of Europe and the USA. Although he is considered pre-eminent by West German modern jewelers and by jewelers all over the world who know of his work, he has had surprisingly few major exhibitions abroad. Many makers have learned – and borrowed – from his jewelry. He has taught many of the most interesting talents, such as Otto Künzli and Daniel Kruger, both of whom are radically different from each other, as well as from Jünger himself. Major restrospective exhibition: Germanisches Nationalmuseum, Nuremberg 1988.

Karpyshin, Richard b. Canada 1955. Studied at the University of Manitoba School of Art; Nova Scotia College of Art and Design. Exhibited in *Jewelry In Transition*, Toronto 1983.

Kasaly, Svatopluk b. Czechoslovakia 1944. Studied at the Vocational School of Glassmaking, Zelenzy Brod School of Applied Arts. Important exhibitions include the *Tendenzen* biennial exhibitions at the Schmuckmuseum, Pforzheim; *Jewelry in Europe*, London 1975.

Knobel, Esther b. Poland 1949. Studied at the Bezalel Academy of Art, Jerusalem; Royal College of Art, London. The striking aspect of her work has been the combination of figuration and decorative abstract pattern. A very few of the pieces have been covertly political, but always the intention is to produce strong, amusing, decorative work that comes alive when worn. Represented in most important group exhibitions, including *Ornamenta 1*, Schmuckmuseum, Pforzheim 1989. Solo exhibitions: The Scottish Gallery, Edinburgh; Galerie Ra, Amsterdam; Galerie Spectrum, Munich. Awarded Françoise van den Bosch Award, Amsterdam 1994.

Koopman, Rena-Beatrice b. USA 1945. Studied at Vassar College, Poughkeepsie, New York, with additional studies in jewelry and sculpture in various institutions.

Kranitzky, Robin *see* **Overstreet, Kim.**

Kruger, Daniel b. South Africa 1951. Studied first as a graphic designer and then went to Munich under Hermann Jünger. Kruger's work is impressive not only for its technical virtuosity but also for its ever-changing imagery. It follows no single theory or aesthetic. He lives and works in Munich and has exhibited widely in West Germany, including *Ornamenta 1*, Schmuckmuseum, Pforzheim 1989; also solo show Galerie Ra, Amsterdam 1993.

Künzli, Otto b. Switzerland 1948. Studied metalwork in Zürich, jewelry in Munich under Hermann Jünger.

Although Künzli can be described as an anti-establishment jeweler, his work is better conceived and crafted than that description might suggest. Its cleverness rests in its ability to subvert conventional decorative jewelry while remaining in itself very attractive. He is one of the most able of the younger modern 'jewelers' and one of those most ill at ease with the values and traditions associated with jewelry. Important solo exhibitions include Schmuckmuseum, Pforzheim 1979; Galerie Ra, Amsterdam 1981; Deutsches Tapetenmuseum, Kassel 1983; Stedelijk Museum, Amsterdam 1991. Currently Professor of Goldsmithing, Akademie der Bildende Künste, Munich.

LaPlantz, David b. USA 1944. Studied metalsmithing at Cranbrook Academy of Art; also a major in art at the College of Education, Bowling Green State University. A hugely energetic jeweler. Works at great speed and is a frequent exhibitor – as well as a constant prizewinner. His students enjoy his teaching. Work in several collections, including the American Craft Museum, New York; Schmuckmuseum, Pforzheim.

Large, Edward de b. UK 1945. Studied at Camberwell School of Art; Royal College of Art, London. Meticulous craftsman, who did much pioneering work with anodizing titanium.

Lechtzin, Stanley b. USA 1936. Studied at Cranbrook Academy of Art; Wayne State University. Professor of Design at Tyler School of Art, Philadelphia, since 1962. An important figure in the development of modern American jewelry. Has exhibited widely in USA and also in Europe.

Leersum, Emmy van Holland 1930–84. Studied at the Instituut voor Kunstnijuerheidsonderwijs, Amsterdam. With her husband Gijs Bakker, she is the most important figure in the recent history of modern jewelry in Holland, though her pioneering, radical and innovative work really falls in the period of the mid-1960s to the mid-1970s. Since then several other figures, with different ideas, have emerged in Holland. She helped to bring together aspects of sculpture, minimalist art and ornament. Exhibited extensively which, together with teaching and study tours throughout Western Europe and the USA, made the Van Leersum/Bakker partnership especially influential. Public collections include Stedelijk Museum, Amsterdam; Victoria and Albert Museum, London; Cleveland Contemporary Jewelry Collection, Middlesbrough. Major retrospective: Museum Het Kruithuis, 's-Hertogenbosch 1993.

Linssen, Nel b. 1935 Holland. Studied Akademie voor Beeldende Kunste, Arnhem. Worked in textile design with systemized patterns and developed a design for a multiple object consisting of flat plastic squares connected by threads that enable infinite arrangements. Further research led to her use of paper, plastic and thread in jewelry. Solo exhibitions held at Galerie Marzee, Nijmegen; Galerie Ra, Amsterdam. Group exhibitions include: *Internationale Schmuckszene '87*, Handwerksmesse, Munich;

Galerie Het Kapelhuis, Amersfoort; *Ornamenta 1*, Schmuckmuseum, Pforzheim; *Paper the Third Dimension*, Aberystwyth Arts Centre, Wales. Public collections: Boymans-van-Beuningen Museum, Rotterdam; Van Reekummuseum, Apeldoorn; Stedelijk Museum, Amsterdam; Cleveland Contemporary Jewelry Collection, Middlesbrough.

Logan, Andrew b. UK 1945. Studied and qualified in architecture at the Oxford School of Architecture. Experimented with surreal interiors and mirror pieces in the 1960s. Initiated *Andrew Logan's Miss World Contest* in 1972. Commissions include: glass-fibre sculptures for Biba's roof garden; props for Mary Quant's exhibition at the Museum of London; Zandra Rhodes fashion shows; set designs for Ballet Rambert and The Royal Ballet. Exhibitions include: *Goldfield Installation*, Whitechapel Art Gallery, London; *Furniture/Sculpture*, Ikon Gallery, Birmingham; *The Maker's Eye*, Crafts Council Gallery, London; *Andrew Logan's Galactic Works*, Limelight, New York; *Andrew Logan's An Artistic Adventure*, MOMA, Oxford (solo show); Opened The Andrew Logan Museum of Sculpture, Berriew, Powys, Wales. Work represented in Cleveland Contemporary Jewelry Collection, Middlesbrough.

Mahlow, Beatrix b. Germany 1957. Studied at the Hochschule der Künste, Berlin; Middlesex Polytechnic, London. Work in the Cleveland Contemporary Jewelry Collection, Middlesbrough.

Maierhofer, Fritz b. Austria 1941. Shown extensively in Europe and was one of the prominent new jewelers of the early and mid-1970s, though his work continues to develop. An influential teacher, represented in various collections, including Schmuckmuseum, Pforzheim. Exhibitions include *Ornamenta 1*, Schmuckmuseum, Pforzheim. Solo: Galerie am Graben, Vienna; Electrum Gallery, London.

Makigawa, Carlier b. 1952 Australia. Studied Curtin University, Western Australia; Royal Melbourne Institute of Technology. Sculptural constructivist interpretations of architecture applied to jewelry with economy and tautness. Principal solo exhibitions: Bonython Gallery, Adelaide; Queen Victoria Museum and Art Gallery, Launceston; Inax Gallery, Tokyo; Helen Drutt Gallery, Philadelphia. Mixed: *Ornamenta 1*, Schmuckmuseum, Pforzheim; *Australian Jewelry*, Galerie Ra, Amsterdam; *The 20th Anniversary Show*, Electrum Gallery, London; *Australia Gold*, South East Asia Tour. Public collections: National Museum of Modern Art, Kyoto; National Gallery, Victoria; Art Gallery of Western Australia; Art Gallery of South Australia; Art Gallery of Queensland; Powerhouse Museum, Sydney.

Manheim, Julia b. UK 1949. Studied Central School of Art, London. One of a group – the others included Caroline Broadhead and Susanna Heron – that emerged from the Central School and that has been in the forefront of new jewelry in the 1970s and 1980s. Now mostly working as a sculptor. Work in public collections, including Crafts

Council, London; Victoria and Albert Museum, London; National Gallery of Victoria, Australia. Cleveland Contemporary Jewelry Collection, Middlesbrough. Contributed to *On the Edge*, Crafts Council Gallery, London 1993.

Martinazzi, Bruno b. Italy 1923. Sculptor and jeweler. Studied first as an industrial chemist, then at the State School of Art, Florence. Important group exhibitions include *Schmuck International 1900–1980*, Vienna 1980; *Jewelry in Europe*, London 1975; *13 Goldsmiths*, Bayerische Akademie der Schönen Künste, Munich 1993.

Marx, Falko b. Germany 1941. Studied Goldschmiedelehre Fachhochschule, Cologne. Amongst the most eclectic of goldsmiths, imbuing a wide range of unlikely materials with quality. Selected exhibitions: *Schmuck International 1900–1980*, Kunstlerhaus, Vienna; *Ornamenta 1*, Schmuckmuseum, Pforzheim; *Infinite Riches*, Museum of Fine Art, St Petersburg; *Facet 1*, Kunsthal, Rotterdam. Solo exhibitions: Louise Smit Gallery, Amsterdam; Helen Drutt Gallery, Philadelphia.

Mattar, Wilhelm T. b. Germany 1946. Studied jewelry and design at Pforzheim. Opened Galerie Mattar in Cologne, which he owns and runs, in 1979. Has shown his own work in Austria, Belgium, Japan, West Germany and UK. Important group exhibitions include *Schmuck International 1900–1980*, Vienna 1980; *International Jewelry Art Exhibition*, Tokyo 1983. Instrumental in setting up Forum für Schmuck und Design, Cologne 1989.

Mawdsley, Richard b. USA 1945. One of the most interesting of the American jewelers because he has channelled his expert craftsmanship into wholly idiosyncratic styles which have very little to do with modern fine – or applied – art ideas, yet are, none the less, contemporary objects. Work in public collections, including the National Museum of American Art, Smithsonian Institution, Washington D.C.

Metcalf, Bruce b. USA 1949. Studied at Syracuse University and then Tyler School of Art, Philadelphia. Currently Professor of Jewelry/Metals at Kent State University, Ohio. Metcalf is a jeweler, craftsman and sculptor. His work, though clearly quite different to that of Richard Mawdsley, is equally idiosyncratic – even taking into account the diverse range of American decorative art. There is no European counterpart to Metcalf in jewelry, though some of the younger British ornamentalist sculptors would find a common chord. Solo exhibitions include the Heller Gallery, New York 1982; Helen Drutt Gallery, Philadelphia; Perimeter Gallery, Chicago. Exhibitions include: *Ornamenta 1*, Schmuckmuseum, Pforzheim 1989; *Facet 1*, Kunsthal, Rotterdam 1993.

Meyerowitz, Patricia b. UK. Studied jewelry at the Central School of Arts and Crafts, London, 1959–60. Moved to USA in 1970. Has practised jewelry and sculpture since 1962 using a process of unit construction, recycling industrial waste. There is an affinity but no confusion between her jewelry making and sculpture which is set out succinctly in her book *Jewelry and Sculpture through Unit Construction*, published in 1967 by Studio Vista, London. Exhibitions include: Ewan Phillips Gallery, London; Electrum Gallery, London; SITES, USA. Solo exhibition: Victoria and Albert Museum, London, where her work is represented.

Nele, E. R. b. West Germany. Studied at the Central School of Art, London 1950–55. Has exhibited widely in Europe and also participated in international exhibitions such as the *1st International Exhibition of Modern Jewelry*, London 1961, and *Schmuck International, 1900–1980*, Vienna 1980.

Niczewski, Peter b. UK 1948. Studied graphics at the Chelsea School of Art, London. Exhibitions include *Jewelry Redefined*, London 1982. Work shown in Galerie Ra, Amsterdam; Aspects, London; Crafts Council, Gallery, London, whose lift interior he also designed.

Ommen, Joke van b. Holland 1948. Studied art history and architecture; private student of goldsmiths Erika Leitner and Peter Skubic. Currently teaching in the USA; the 'Dutch style' of her work has become modified into a noticeably American idiom. Exhibitions include *Schmuck International, 1900–1980*, Vienna 1980; *Jewelry Redefined*, London 1982; *Good As Gold*, Washington D.C. 1981 and USA tour.

Overstreet, Kim b. USA 1955. Studied Virginia Western Community College.

Kranitzky, Robin b. USA 1956. Studied Virginia Commonwealth University.

Kranitzky and Overstreet join forces to create the most fantastic narrative jewelry. Some work reads like entries in a personal diary or illustrations from a book of fairytales. Selected exhibitions: *Whimsy*, Elaine Potter Gallery, San Francisco; *Ancient Inspirations*, Carlyn Gallery, New York; *The Primitive Image*, Ferrin Gallery, North Hampton; *American Dreams, American Extremes*, Museum Het Kruithuis, 's-Hertogenbosch; *Beauty is a Story*, Museum Het Kruithuis, 's-Hertogenbosch.

Paley, Albert R., Jr. b. USA 1944. Studied sculpture at Tyler School of Art, Temple University, Philadelphia. Exhibited in major international exhibitions of jewelry, but is now an internationally acclaimed blacksmith working on architectural commissions. Work is in many collections, including the Renwick Gallery, Washington D.C.

Petry, Michael b. USA 1960. Studied art and mathematics, Rice University, Houston, Texas. Multi-media performance artist.

Planteydt, Annelies b. Holland 1956. Studied at the Gerrit Rietveld Akademie, Amsterdam. Work shown in Galerie Cada, Munich; Galerie Ra, Amsterdam.

Poston, David b. USSR 1948, UK citizen. Studied at Hornsey College of Art and Design, London. Exhibited in Europe and Australia. One of the first jewelers to use textiles in his work. Represented in Crafts Council Collection, London,

where he curated *What is Jewelry*, an investigative exhibition, in 1994.

Quigley, Robin L. b. USA 1947. Studied at Tyler School of Art, Temple University, Philadelphia; Rhode Island School of Design. Important solo exhibitions include the Helen Drutt Gallery, Philadelphia, 1978 and 1981. Shows also at Galerie Ra, Amsterdam. Work in collections including Tyler School of Art; the Helen Drutt Gallery.

Ramshaw, Wendy b. UK 1939. Trained in illustration and fabric design; self-taught jeweler. Her collections of rings, often grouped together on lathe-turned miniature acrylic minarets, created a lot of interest in modern jewelry circles in the early 1970s. The bulk of her work continues to be well crafted in precious metals. She has exhibited widely and frequently all over the world and has work in many collections, including Victoria and Albert Museum, London; Schmuckmuseum, Pforzheim. Awarded OBE 1993.

Reiling, Reinhold b. Germany 1922, d. 1983. A highly influential jeweler, assured of an important place in the history of 20th-century European jewelry. It goes without saying that, as a leading West German jeweler, his craftsmanship was superb, but so too was his design sense. His most recent solo exhibition was at the Schmuckmuseum, Pforzheim 1982 – and his work is in the Schmuckmuseum's collection.

Rezac, Susan b. Czechoslovakia 1953, Swiss citizen. Studied sculpture at the Rhode Island School of Design, USA. Shows with Helen Drutt Gallery, USA.

Roberts, Geoff b. UK 1953. Studied sculpture at Birmingham College of Art and printmaking at the Royal College of Art, London. The lightweight qualities of printed acrylic, with its metallic finish, enable Roberts to work on a large scale, from which his ideas for production work derive. Exhibitions include: *The Maker's Eye*, Crafts Council Gallery, London; *Jewelry Redefined*, Contemporary Applied Arts, London; *Internationale Schmuckszene '87*, Handwerksmesse, Munich; *All that Glisters ...*, The British Council; *Paper to Platinum*, Lesley Craze Gallery, London.

Rössle, Annette b. Germany 1951. Studied under Hermann Jünger. Has exhibited in West Germany, but now owns and runs the Galerie Cada, Munich.

Roth, Kobi b. Israel 1962. Studied Bezalel Academy of Art, Jerusalem. Exhibitions: *Aggression in Jewelry*, Forum für Schmuck und Design, Cologne; Internationale Schmuckszene '92', Handwerksmesse, Munich. Prize: American-Israel Cultural Foundation.

Rothmann, Gerd b. Germany 1941. Studied at the Staatliche Zeichenakademie, Hanau. Worked in Hermann Jünger's studio in 1966. Several solo and international group exhibitions, including some early group shows of importance (e.g. with Claus Bury and Fritz Maierhofer at Electrum, London 1972). One of the first jewelers to use acrylics. Continues link with Electrum (e.g. innovative body-works exhibition there in 1982). Work included in various collections, including Schmuckmuseum, Pforzheim.

ROY b. USA 1962. Studied Carnegie Mellon University, Pittsburgh. Recycling street signs, this designer builds her cityscape collages, combining the street hardware irreverently with diamonds and rubies. Selected exhibitions: *Born with a Silver Spoon*, National Ornamental Metal Museum, Memphis, Tennessee; *The Domestic Object*, The Berkshire Museum, Pittsfield, Massachusetts. Solo exhibition: Gallery 525, St Louis.

Sajet, Philip b. Holland 1953. Studied Gerrit Rietveld Akademie, Amsterdam. A goldsmith who turns a vice into a virtue, with an inconsistency of styles that mixes design metaphors and materials. Sajet's *Homage to Francis Bacon*, a long chain necklace with a quote wrought in gold, has become famous. Selected exhibitions: *Ornamenta 1*, Schmuckmuseum, Pforzheim; *Beauty is a Story*, Museum Het Kruithuis, 's-Hertogenbosch; *Facet 1*, Kunsthal, Rotterdam. Solo exhibitions: Galerie Ra, Amsterdam; Louise Smit Gallery, Amsterdam; Galerie für Modernen Schmuck, Frankfurt; Galerie Mattar, Cologne; Galerie Neon, Brussels.

Sarneel, Lucy b. Holland, 1961. Studied at the Municipal Academy, Maastricht; Gerrit Rietveld Akademie, Amsterdam. Uses jewelry as a subject to explore social issues. Exhibitions include: *Jugend Gestaltet*, Handwerksmesse, Munich; *Beauty is a Story*, Museum Het Kruithuis, 's-Hertogenbosch; *Facet 1*, Kunsthal, Rotterdam. Solo exhibition: Galerie Marzee, Nijmegen.

Schick, Marjorie b. USA 1941. Studied at the University of Wisconsin; Indiana University; Sir John Cass School, London. A very innovative maker – and her work of the last twenty years gives the lie to the idea that all the radical work of recent decades has been European. Shows with Galerie Ra, Amsterdam; Aspects Gallery, London.

Scott, Ann b. USA 1959. Studied at Moore College of Art, Philadelphia. Group exhibitions include Helen Drutt Gallery, Philadelphia.

Selkirk, David b. Australia 1954. Studied at Western Australian Institute of Technology. Exhibited in numerous group shows in Australia. Exhibited in *Jewelry Redefined*, London 1982; *Australian Jewelry*, Tokyo 1983.

Sharlin, Miriam b. USA 1952. Studied at Bennington College, Bennington, Vermont; State University of New York, New Paltz, New York. A meticulous craftswoman whose work has been influenced by West German goldsmiths. She has had several solo exhibitions in the USA and West Germany, as well as being represented in most of the important international group exhibitions. Her work can be seen in the Schmuckmuseum, Pforzheim.

Shirk, Helen b. USA 1942. Studied at Skidmore College, New York; Kunsthaandvaerkerskolen, Copenhagen; Indiana University. Currently Professor of Art, San Diego State University. Exhibitions include *Tendenzen*, Pforzheim 1982; *Good As Gold*, Washington D.C. 1981 and USA tour; *Black Jewelry*, Oxford 1981. Work in public collections, including Indiana University Fine Arts Museum; University of Texas.

Skal, Hubertus von b. Czechoslovakia 1942, lives in Munich. Studied at the Akademie der Bildenden Künste, Munich. Exhibited widely in Europe and work shown in the USA. Has always been highly respected by fellow jewelers even when, as in the late 1970s, his fine workmanship in precious materials was outside the mainstream of contemporary jewelry. Recent international group shows include *Schmuck International 1900–1980*, Vienna 1980; *Tendenzen*, Pforzheim 1982.

Smit, Robert b. Holland 1941. Studied at Technische School voor Delft en Omstreken; Staatliche Kunst und Werkschule, Pforzheim. Selected solo exhibitions: Stedelijk Museum, Amsterdam; Galerie Philip Debray, Rihimäki, Finland; *Towards the Liberation of Drawings*, a series of ten solo exhibitions at Galerie Orez Mobiel, The Hague; Spectrum Gallery, Munich; Galerie Ra, Amsterdam. Selected group exhibitions: Galerie Nouvelles Images, The Hague; *Jewelry in Europe*, Victoria and Albert Museum, London; *Triennale du Bijou*, Musée des Arts Décoratifs, Paris; *Facet 1*, Kunsthal, Rotterdam.

Spiller, Eric b. UK 1946. Studied at the Central School of Art, London. His work is among the 'quietest' of that produced by the new innovative jewelers – very well made, precisely designed. Exhibited in Europe, USA, Australia. Work in public collections, including Crafts Council, London; the Worshipful Company of Goldsmiths, London.

Stewart, Gordon b. UK 1963. Studied at Glasgow School of Art; Royal College of Art, London (under David Watkins). Stewart's jewelry chronicles his background, with photographs taken from the family album and transferred onto anodized metal that is 'distressed' – bringing a faded, nostalgic effect. These personal memoirs owe a small debt to miniature portraiture. Exhibitions include: *Internationale Schmuckszene '89*, Handwerksmesse, Munich; *Constructions in Jewelry and Metal Objects*, Oriel Gallery, Cardiff; *Edinburgh Salutes Glasgow*, The Scottish Gallery, Edinburgh; *British Jewelry*, Crafts Council Gallery, London. Stewart is a member of Flux – Glasgow Fine Metal Group. Public collections: Crafts Council Collection, London; Cleveland Contemporary Jewelry Collection, Middlesbrough.

Stofer, Hans b. Switzerland 1957. Qualified as an engineer in Switzerland before studying design at Zurich School of Art. Lived in the UK since 1987. In the *New Metalwork* exhibition at Contemporary Applied Arts in 1993, Stofer showed some original thinking with a collection of 'fruit cages': black wire constructions punning the fruit bowl. These witty objects, designed to take specific groups of fruit, heightened the perception of colour and form with piercing clarity. Exhibitions include: Galerie am Graben, Vienna; V&V, Vienna; The Scottish Gallery, Edinburgh; Musée Decoratifs, Geneva. His work has been bought by the Contemporary Arts Society, London.

Tamminen, Olli b. Finland 1944. Graduated as an industrial designer and jeweler from the Institute of Industrial Arts in Helsinki, where he has taught at the university. Balance is the generating force behind Tamminen's sensitive handling of materials, which are given equal status to produce his tactile pendulums for the body. Exhibitions include: *Finnish Design*, Museum of Applied Arts, Helsinki; *Scandinavia Today*, Tokyo and New York; *Internationale Schmuckszene '88*, Handwerksmesse, Munich; V&V, Vienna; Artek, Helsinki. Public collections: Museum of Modern Art, New York; Museum of Applied Arts, Helsinki; Museum of Applied Arts, Budapest.

Taylor, Jared b. UK 1966. Studied at Duncan of Jordanstone College of Art, Dundee; Royal College of Art, London. Architecture and old technology feature as sources of inspiration in Taylor's large-scale work, transposed into light, wearable ornament through the use of plastics and resins. Exhibitions include: Wilson & Gough, London; Worshipful Company of Goldsmiths, London; Compass Gallery, Glasgow; *Internationale Schmuckszene '92*, Handwerksmesse, Munich, where he was awarded the Hermann-Hoffmann Prize. His work features in the Cleveland Contemporary Jewelry Collection, Middlesbrough.

Thomas, Detlef b. Germany 1959. Studied at the Goldschmiedelehre, Cologne; Akademie der Bildenden Künste, Munich (under Hermann Jünger). Original interpretations of constructivist principles applied with economy to jewelry, prior to more formal organic styles. Exhibitions include: *Ornamenta 1*, Schmuckmuseum, Pforzheim; *Triennale Européenne du Bijou*, Musée du Luxembourg, Paris; *Constructions in Jewelry*, Oriel Gallery, Cardiff; *Beauty is a Story*, Museum Het Kruithuis, 's-Hertogenbosch; *Facet 1*, Kunsthal, Rotterdam. Solo exhibition: Galerie für Modernen Schmuck, Frankfurt. Hermann-Hoffmann Prize, Munich, 1989.

Tipler, Adele b. UK 1970. Studied Barnsley College of Art & Design; Wolverhampton Polytechnic; Royal College of Art, London. Electroformed headpieces of organic design, which marry jewelry disciplines with industrial techniques to create lightweight structures in copper and other metals. Exhibitions: *Young Designers*, Business Design Centre, London; Galerie Marzee, Nijmegen; *Young Makers*, Crafts Council Gallery, London.

Tisdale, David b. USA 1956. Studied design at the University of California; San Diego State University. Exhibited widely in California and abroad, including *Four American Jewelers*, Vienna 1983. Work shown at Galerie Ra, Amsterdam.

Vigeland, Tone b. Norway 1938. Studied at the National College of Art, Craft and Design, and at the Technical College, Oslo. Established her own studio there in 1961. Recognized internationally as a leading figure in twentieth-century jewelry design. During the past ten years or so,

Vigeland has attracted further attention for work that expands Scandinavian reductivist design principles. Building layers of unit construction, she achieves some intriguing effects that contrast the light, shade and depth of materials, sometimes reminiscent of armoury. Solo exhibitions include: Kunstindustrimuseet, Oslo; Electrum Gallery, London; Artwear, New York; Helen Drutt Gallery, Philadelphia. Vigeland's work is represented in many international collections, including: Cooper-Hewitt Museum, New York; Museum of Modern Art, New York; National Museum of Modern Art, Tokyo; Nationalmuseum, Stockholm; Schmuckmuseum, Pforzheim; Victoria and Albert Museum, London; Musée des Arts Décoratifs, Paris; Kunstindustrimuseet, Oslo.

Waldow, von, Wolf b. Germany 1962. Studied industrial design at the Kunsthochschule, Hamburg. Jewelry that confronts gay sexual orientation and issues surrounding conventions of masculinity. Solo exhibition: Galerie Ra, Amsterdam.

Walker, David b. UK 1941. Studied Manchester College of Art & Design. Emigrated to Australia in 1964. Currently Head of Jewelry and Metalwork, Curtin University, Perth. Selected solo exhibitions: Queen Victoria Museum and Art Gallery, Launceston; Contemporary Jewelry Gallery, Sydney. Mixed: *Decade of Craft in Western Australia*, Crafts Council Gallery, Perth; *The Australian Experience*, Contemporary Jewelry Gallery, Sydney; *Perth International Crafts Triennial*, Art Gallery of Western Australia.

Watkins, David b. UK 1940. Studied sculpture at the University of Reading. Jazz musician. Exhibited widely in Europe, USA and Australia. His work over the last ten years presents one of the most consistent catalogues of thoughtful design and development in new jewelry. Work in public collections, including the Crafts Council, London; Worshipful Company of Goldsmiths, London. Currently Professor of Goldsmithing, Silversmithing and Jewelry, Royal College of Art, London.

Weber, Norman b. Germany 1964. Studied at the Staatliche Berufsfachschule für Glas und Schmuck, Neugablonz; Akademie der Bildenden Künste, Munich (under Otto Künzli). Witty and cynical interpretations of mass-produced jewelry. Selected exhibitions: Kunstmuseum, Düsseldorf; Städtische Galerie, Lenbachhaus, Munich; *Facet 1*, Kunsthal, Rotterdam.

Wehrens, Jan b. Holland 1945. Studied in Holland and West Germany, and now works in Munich. His work is closely associated with clothing – making allusions to buckles or epaulettes, for example – but combined with the decorative aspect is a hard, almost 'militaristic' image.

Wippermann, Andrea b. Germany 1963. Studied at Burg Giebichenstein Hochschule für Kunst und Design, Halle (under Renate Heintze and Dorothea Prühl). Selected exhibitions: Galerie Metallform, Berlin; Handwerksform Hanover Kunst und Form; *Schmuck Burg Giebichenstein*

1970–1992, Museum des Kunsthandwerks, Grassimuseum, Leipzig, 1993.

Woell, Fred b. USA 1934. Studied at the University of Illinois; University of Wisconsin; Cranbrook Academy of Art. An influential figure in American jewelry and known for his early satirical pieces. Work in public collections, including the American Craft Museum, New York; Helen Drutt Gallery, Philadelphia. Widely exhibited throughout the USA and a noted teacher and lecturer.

Wood, Joe b. USA 1954. Studied Kent State University, SUNY College, Buffalo. A leading exponent of new innovative jewelry in the USA, with leanings towards Post-Modernism. Selected exhibitions: *The Art of Jewelry*, Setagaya Museum, Tokyo; *The Body Adorned*, Fox Fine Arts Center, University of Texas; *Crossroads*, Artwear Gallery, New York; *Internationale Schmuckszene '91*, Handwerksmesse, Munich; *Ornamenta 1*, Schmuckmuseum, Pforzheim.

Wolf, Lam de b. Holland 1949. Studied textiles at the Gerrit Rietveld Akademie, Amsterdam. Her textile constructions and 'garments' are almost theatrical and, if not conventional jewelry, are certainly in the category of body ornament. In a curious way, she ventures into the anti-Modernist style of ornament that is finding favour with younger interior and fashion designers in Western Europe. Her work has been exhibited widely in Holland and Britain and is included in the collection of Mr and Mrs Knapp, New York.

Zahn, Helga b. Germany (1936–85). Came to England in 1957 and studied at Leeds College of Art; Central School of Art and Crafts, London. Taught Leicester College of Art; Basic Research Unit, Summer School, New York; Haystack School of Art, Maine, USA; Hornsey College of Art, London. Zahn's work and personality was a significant influence in British jewelry during the 1960s and 1970s. Her unsentimental graphic interpretations of nature and the use of natural materials were matched by an ambitious and strong sense of scale, colour and line. Exhibitions included: *The Goldsmith Today*, Goldsmiths Hall, London; *Tendenzen '70*, Schmuckmuseum, Pforzheim; *Opening Exhibition*, Electrum Gallery, London; *Jewelry in Europe*, V&A and UK tour. Major retrospective exhibition: Crafts Advisory Committee (now Crafts Council), London. Public collections: Schmuckmuseum, Pforzheim; Worshipful Company of Goldsmiths, London; National Museum of Wales, Cardiff; Crafts Council Collection, London. Gold Medal: Internationale Handwerksmesse, Munich, 1966.

GALLERIES AND MUSEUMS

Specialist, independent gallery directors have been crucial in the development of new art-jewelry. Such directors have had to be especially adventurous because the audience and the market for innovative work is still young. Yet independent galleries are succeeding, as well as surviving, and their role is important even in countries such as Britain and America where there are well-established public institutions supporting the crafts. In practice the independent galleries have been prepared to risk first showings of new talent, while the subsidized gallery directors usually need to have an eye on the demands of those who represent the interests of trustees or taxpayers.

The difference between a shop and a gallery is more than a difference of degree. A shop may well sell good work, but a gallery tries to develop a point of view. In a way a gallery is like a very good critic – you may not always agree with the stance or the conclusion but you can trust them because a policy and a consistent philosophy has been developed.

However, the subsidized galleries and museums have also become important, partly because – when they deal with jewelry – they can afford to be singleminded and don't have to compromise to make money (none but the most rigorous of the independent galleries specialize wholly in innovative art-jewelry). Equally, public institutions have the resources for good presentation and scholarship through well-researched leaflets and catalogues. A wider public is also reached through better, more professional promotional facilities.

There is some argument – it has been quite acrimonious in Britain, which has a substantial support system for art, craft, design and film – as to whether or not state subsidies encourage makers to forget the interests of the buying public. The criticism has been that by being provided with grants and exhibitions (which may lead to teaching posts in art schools) the makers have had very little need to sell their work: their work, their 'art', has therefore become introspective and of interest to fellow makers but not to others. There is some truth in this argument, but none the less the partnership between the state and independent galleries is encouraging a wider audience of informed people wanting and willing to buy jewelry which they might first have become aware of through the subsidized sector. New jewelry needs the vigour of the independent galleries to discover talent and sell it, while the public sector is required to consolidate reputations and maintain quality.

Among the key modern jewelry galleries Paul Derrez's *Galerie Ra* is one of the most important influences on jewelry in Holland and Britain. Galerie Ra's work has also prompted strong interest among connoisseurs elsewhere in Europe and in the United States. Its particular interpretation of modernism, with an emphasis upon non-precious jewelry that rejects the notion that jewelry must always declare status and position, runs counter to certain strong characteristics in West German, Austrian and American work. It is nevertheless true that Galerie Ra shows a wide range of jewelers.

Galleries are made by the people who run them and in Britain modern jewelry has been much helped by individuals, including Graham Hughes (who for a long time worked for the Worshipful Company of Goldsmiths, London), Ralph Turner and Barbara Cartlidge. In 1971, for example, Barbara Cartlidge and Ralph Turner founded the *Electrum Gallery* in London. The early 1970s saw a number of very important exhibitions at Electrum, with several major shows of European jewelers across a spectrum from Emmy van Leersum and Gijs Bakker to Hubertus von Skal. Ralph Turner left to become Head of Exhibitions at the Crafts Council, London, and Barbara Cartlidge continues to run Electrum with a stable of makers that includes Wendy Ramshaw and Frank Bauer.

In the United States of America the *Helen Drutt Gallery*, Philadelphia, is of much importance because it has shown many hitherto unknown makers from both Europe and the USA. Helen Drutt believes it is essential that a gallery should develop a point of view, and that the director should act as an editor, even a tastemaker. Her attitude to the relationship between fashion and jewelry, however, is not espoused by some of the other gallery owners in America dealing in modern jewelry. In an interesting round up of American gallery directors' views (*Metalsmith* magazine, Winter 1984), several directors agreed with Robert Lee Morris, director of *Art Wear*, New York, when he said: 'It is good to be influenced by fashion trends in order to stay current and not repeat what has already been done.' Helen Drutt, like Paul Derrez or Wilhelm Mattar of *Galerie Mattar* in Cologne, West Germany, concentrates on longer-term developments in aesthetics. But, of course, the fashion aspect of new jewelry plays up to fashion-conscious, as well as design-conscious, people. There can be no hard-and-fast 'ideologies' in any of the decorative arts, and certainly not in jewelry.

The independent galleries and public museums listed below reflect the balance of entrepreneurial innovation and establishment endorsement outlined above. This list is by no means exhaustive, but it does present a good range of reliable, high-quality galleries and museums.

Australia

Art Gallery of South Australia, North Terrace, Adelaide 5000, South Australia
The Western Australian Art Gallery, Beaufort Street, Perth 6000, Western Australia
National Gallery of Victoria, Victoria Arts Centre, 180 St Kilda Road, Melbourne 3000, Victoria.

These are state-assisted galleries, building collections of new Australian, European and American work.

Austria

Galerie am Graben, Graben 7, A-1010 Vienna
Galerie V & V, Lindengasse 5, A-1070 Vienna

Both galleries have lively modern exhibitions. Galerie am Graben is the longer established of the two, with a particular historical strength in Art Nouveau.

Belgium

Galerie Neon, 19 Rue Defacqz, 1050 Brussels
Galerie Sofie Lachaert, Zwartezustersstraat 20, 9000 Gent
Villa de Bondt: New Jewels Gallery, Krijgslaan 124, 9000 Gent

Canada

Galerie Jocelyne Gobeil, 2154 rue Crescent, Montreal
Prime Canadian Crafts, 229 Queen Street W, Toronto

Germany

Atelier AKUT, Südstrasse 10, 4150 Krefeld
D'OR, Herbartgang 11, 2900 Oldenburg
Forum für Schmuck und Design, Lüttigerstrasse 47, W-5000 Cologne
Galerie Cada, Hans-Sachs-Strasse 11, D-8000 Munich 5
Galerie Feinschmiede, Windscheidstrasse 24, 1000 Berlin 12
Galerie für Modernen Schmuck, Weckmarket 3, 6 Frankfurt
Galerie Mattar, Lüttigerstrasse 46, 5 Cologne 1
Galerie Orferre, Bastionstrasse 31, 4000 Düsseldorf
Galerie Rehklau, Alte Gasse 11, 89001 Augsburg

Galerie Spectrum, Türkenstrasse 97, D-8000 Munich 40
Galerie Trykorn, Savignyplatz 13 Passage, 1000 Berlin 12
Galerie Ventil, Kirchenstrasse 69, D-8000 Munich 80
The Goldschmiedehaus, Altstadter Markt 6, Hanau am Main 645
The Hessiches Landesmuseum, Friedenplatz, 61 Darmstadt
Museum für Kunst und Gewerbe, 1 Steintorplatz, Hamburg 2
Schmuckmuseum Pforzheim im Reuchlinhaus, Jahnstrasse 42, Pforzheim 753
Sternthaler, Ermekeilstrasse 16, 5300 Bonn 1
Werkstattgalerie, Meierottostrasse 1, 1000 Berlin 15

Since it is the only museum of jewelry, the Schmuckmuseum at Pforzheim is important, as are its biennial *Tendenzen* exhibitions. The smaller, commercial galleries, such as Cada, Spectrum and Mattar, show very good modern work by jewelers from all over Europe and the USA. The Museum für Kunst und Gewerbe contains a variety of twentieth-century work, as does the Hessiches Landesmuseum (with its noted Art Nouveau collection) which also stages international exhibitions of modern jewelry. The Forum für Schmuck und Design is an association that circulates information on jewelry's international activities through its journal, exhibitions calendar and broadsheets. Occasionally the Forum holds summer workshops and arranges studio visits and conferences (address above).

Holland

Beeld en Aambeeld, Walstraat 33, 7511 GE Enschede
Den Bosch, Gemeente Museum, Arnhem
Flora Design, Grote Berg 1A, Eindhoven
Galerie De Sluis, Sluiskant 24, 22645 AB Leidschendam
Galerie Eewal, Eewal 84, 8911 GV Leeuwarden
Galerie Marzee, Lange Hezelstraat 19, 6511 CA Nijmegen
Galerie Nouvelles Images, Westeinde 22, 2512 HD, The Hague
Galerie Ra, Vijzelstraat 80, 1017 HL Amsterdam
Galerie Serafÿn, Minrebroederstraat 1, Utrecht
Louise Smit Gallery, Prinsengracht 615, 1016 HT, Amsterdam
Museum Het Kruithuis, 's-Hertogenbosch
Stedelijk Museum, Paulus Porterstraat 13, 5082 Amsterdam

The Van Reekummuseum, Koninginnelaan 9, 7315 BJ Apeldoorn

Galerie Ra and Galerie Louise Smit are independent galleries showing top quality new jewelry. The various museums are building important collections of modern jewelry, with an emphasis upon European work.

Switzerland
Byou Terrible, Zollikerstrasse 14, 8008 Zürich
Galleria Cubo, Via Maraini 27, CH 6900 Lugano
Galerie Michele Zeller, Kramgasse 20, 3011 Bern

UK
Argenta, 82 Fulham Road, London SW3
Argosy Gallery and Bookshop, 2 Abbey Green, Bath BA1, Avon
Barclaycraft, 7 East Street, Brighton, Sussex
The Chestnut Gallery, High Street, Bourton-on-the-Water, Gloucestershire
Cleveland Crafts Centre, 57 Gilkes Street, Middlesbrough, Cleveland
Contemporary Applied Arts, 43 Earlham Street, London WC2
Crafts Centre & Design Gallery, Leeds City Art Gallery, The Headrow, Leeds, West Yorkshire
Craft Centre, Royal Exchange Theatre, St Ann's Square, Manchester
Crafts Council Gallery, 44a Pentonville Road, Islington, London N1 9BY
Dartington Craft Shop, Ciderpress Gallery, Shinners Bridge, Dartington, Totnes, Devon
Electrum Gallery, 21 South Molton Street, London W1
Facets, 14 Broadstone, Dartmouth, Devon
Focus Gallery, 108 Derby Road, Nottingham
Katherine House Gallery, The Parade, Marlborough, Wiltshire
Lesley Craze Gallery, 34 Clerkenwell Green, London EC1
The Midland Group Shop, 24–32 Carlton Street, Nottingham
New Ashgate Gallery, Downing Street, Farnham, Surrey
New Craftsman, 24 Fore Street, St Ives, Cornwall
Oriel Gallery, The Friary, Cardiff
Oxford Gallery, 23 High Street, Oxford
Roger Billcliffe fine art, 134 Blythswood Street, Glasgow
The Scottish Crafts Centre, 140 Cannongate, Royal Mile, Edinburgh
The Scottish Gallery, 16 Dundas Street, Edinburgh

Victoria and Albert Museum, South Kensington, London SW7
Wilson and Gough, 106 Draycott Avenue, London SW3
Worshipful Company of Goldsmiths, Goldsmiths Hall, Foster Lane EC2

The Crafts Council, London, publish an annual free map, listing selected shops and galleries in the UK. The map is available on request. The Victoria and Albert Museum is Britain's museum of the decorative arts; new jewelry is a small but serious part of the institution's interest. The Worshipful Company of Goldsmiths has a history going back 800 years, but has an important collection of modern jewelry. Since 1984, Cleveland County Council in north-east England has been building an international collection of contemporary jewelry. Seen primarily as an educational aid, the collection has been curated from its inception by Ralph Turner. Representing many of the principal names on jewelry design, it is one of the few international collections of contemporary work in the UK. The collection is managed by the Cleveland Crafts Centre, Middlesbrough, and the jewelry can be seen on application.

USA
The American Craft Museum, 73 W 45th Street, New York, NY 10019
Betsy Rosenfield Gallery, 212 W. Superior, Chicago, IL 60610
Blue Streak Gallery, Inc, 1723 Delaware Avenue, Wilmington, DE 19806
Byzantium, 105 Thompson Street, New York, NY 10012
Concepts, 6th & Mission Street, Carmel, CA 93921
Contemporary Artisans Gallery, 530 Bush Street, San Francisco, CA 94108
Contemporary Crafts, 3934 S.W. Corbett Avenue, Portland, OR 97201
Convergence, 484 Broome Street, New York, NY 10013
Cooper-Hewitt Museum of Decorative Arts and Design, Smithsonian Institution, 9 E. 90th Street, New York, NY 10019
Craftsman's Gallery, 16 Chase Road, Scarsdale, NY 10583
Detail, 204 Spring Street, New York, NY 10012
Elizabeth Fortner Gallery, 1114 State Street, Studio 9-La Arcada Court, Santa Barbara, CA 93101
Etienne, 20 Main Street, Camden, ME 04843
Freehand, 8413 W. 3rd Street, Los Angeles, CA 90048

Gallery Eight, 7464 Girard Avenue, La Jolla, CA 92037
Gallery 10, 21 Greenwich Avenue, New York, NY 10014
Gayle Willson Gallery, 42b Jobs Lane, Southampton, NY 11968
Graham Gallery, 908 Prospect St, La Jolla CA 92037
Handcrafters Gallery, 44 Exchange Street, Portland, ME 04101
Helen Drutt Gallery, 1721 Walnut Street, Philadelphia, PA 19103
Jackie Chalkley Gallery, 3301 New Mexico Avenue N.W., Washington, D.C. 20016
Maple Hill Gallery, 367 Fore Street, Portland, ME 04101
Merritt Gallery, 800 Powers Building, Rochester, NY 14614
Mindscape, 1521 Sherman Avenue, Evanston, IL 60201
Perception Galleries, 1724 Bissonnet, Houston, TX 77005
Plum Gallery, 3762 Howard Avenue, Kensington, MD 20895
Renwick Gallery of the National Museum of American Art (Smithsonian Institution), Pennsylvania Avenue at 17th Street N.W., Washington, D.C. 20560
Sheila Nussbaum Gallery, 358 Millburn Avenue, Millburn, NJ 07041
A Singular Place, 2718 Main Street, Santa Monica, CA 90405
Spring Street Enamels Gallery, 171 Spring Street, New York, NY. 10012
Swan Galleries, 8433 Germantown Avenue, Philadelphia, PA 19118
Ten Arrow, Ten Arrow Street, Cambridge, MA 02138
V O Galerie – Contemporary Jewelry, 2000 Pennsylvania Avenue, Washington, D.C. 20006
Westminster Gallery, 132A Newbury Street, Boston, MA 02116
Whichcraft, 52 Vose Avenue, South Orange, NJ 07079

There are a great many craft shops, galleries, museums and public collections throughout the USA and interested viewers are urged to contact such organizations as the American Craft Council, 401 Park Avenue South, New York, NY 10016 or the Society of North American Goldsmiths, University of South Illinois, Carbondale, Illinois. The Renwick Gallery is especially important since it is intended to function as a national gallery for American design and the decorative arts. The American Craft Museum has regular exhibitions, some of which are given to national or foreign new jewelry exhibitions.

EXHIBITIONS

A selected list of important exhibitions with catalogues

1961 *1st International Exhibition of Modern Jewelry*, Worshipful Company of Goldsmiths, London

1963 *Modern British Jewelry*, Worshipful Company of Goldsmiths, London

1965 *Internationale Ausstellung Schmuck*, Hessisches Landesmuseum, Darmstadt, West Germany

1966 Friedrich Becker, Worshipful Company of Goldsmiths, London

1967 *Tendenzen*, Schmuckmuseum, Pforzheim, West Germany – first of an international biennial series still continuing

1969 *Objects to Wear* (Van Leersum, Bakker, Van Beek, Van der Bosch, Lameris), Van Abbemuseum, Eindhoven, Holland; then USA tour

1970 *International Exhibition of Jewelry*, Tokyo – first of an international triennial series still continuing

1970 Gerda Flöckinger, Victoria and Albert Museum, London

1972 *Sieraad 1900–1972*, Zonnehof Museum, Amersfoort, Holland

1972 Rüdiger Lorenzen, Schmuckmuseum, Pforzheim, West Germany

1973 *British Jewelry*, Electrum Gallery, London; then Holland tour

1973 *The Craftsman's Art*, Crafts Advisory Committee (now Crafts Council), London

1974 Claus Bury, Schmuckmuseum, Pforzheim, West Germany

1974 *Schmuck Aus Stahl*, International Symposium, Vienna

1975 *On Tour – Ten British Jewelers*, Crafts Council, London. Toured West Germany and Australia

1975 *Contemporary Crafts of America.* Toured USA

1975 *Jewelry in Europe*, Victoria and Albert Museum, London; then UK tour

1976 *Jewelry of Margaret de Patta*, Oakland, California, USA

1976 *Loot*, Worshipful Company of Goldsmiths, London – first of an annual series still continuing

1978 Claus Bury, Hermann Jünger, Gerd Rothmann, Hessiches Landesmuseum, Darmstadt, West Germany

1979 Otto Künzli, Schmuckmuseum, Pforzheim, West Germany

1980 *Schmuck International 1900–1980*, Kunstlerhaus, Vienna

1980 Emmy van Leersum Retrospective, Stedelijk Museum, Amsterdam

1980 Susanna Heron, *Bodywork*, Crafts Council, London

1981 Caroline Broadhead, Arnolfini Gallery, Bristol, UK

1981 Hermann Jünger, Galerie am Graben, Vienna

1981 *Ready Made*, Galerie Mattar, Cologne, West Germany

1981 *Beyond Tradition*, American Craft Museum, New York

1981 *Good as Gold*, Renwick Gallery, Smithsonian Institution, Washington D.C.; then USA tour

1982 *Jewelry Redefined*, International Exhibition, British Crafts Centre, London; then European tour

1982 Pierre Degen, *New Work*, Crafts Council, London

1982 Fritz Maierhofer, Galerie am Graben, Vienna

1982 *Views on Jewelry 1965–1982*, Stedelijk Museum, Amsterdam

1982 Reinhold Reiling, Schmuckmuseum, Pforzheim, West Germany

1983 Otto Künzli, Deutsches Tapetenmuseum, Kassel, West Germany

1983 *The Jewelry Project* (Knapp Collection), Crafts Council, London – the private collection of Mr and Mrs Knapp, New York

1983 *New Departures in British Jewelry*, American Craft Museum, New York; then USA tour

1984 Daniel Kruger, Schmuckmuseum, Pforzheim, West Germany

1984 *Some Dutch Jewelry*, Arnolfini Gallery, Bristol, UK

1984 *Contemporary Jewelry*, the Americas, Australia, Europe and Japan, Museum of Modern Art, Kyoto

1984 *Cross Currents*, jewelry from Australia, Britain, Germany, Holland, Power House Museum, Sydney

1984 *Jewelry, Austrian Contemporary Art*, Galerie am Graben, Vienna

1984 *Modern Artist Jewels*, Victoria and Albert Museum, London

1984 *Structure & Ornament*, American Modernist Jewelry, 50 FIFTY, New York

1984 Ros Conway, Victoria and Albert Museum, London

1984 Patricia Meyerowitz, Victoria and Albert Museum, London

1984 Daniel Kruger, Schmuckmuseum, Pforzheim

1985 *Jewelry from Britain, Germany, Holland, Belgium*, International Cultural Centre, Antwerp

1986 Gerda Flöckinger, Victoria and Albert Museum, London

1986 *10 Years*, Galerie Ra, Amsterdam

1986 *Craft Today-Poetry of the Physical*, American Crafts Museum, New York

1986 *Robert Smit-Beyond Reach*, Stedelijk Museum, Het Prinsenhof, Delft

1987 *Norwegian Jewelry*, Norwegian Ministry of Foreign Affairs, Oslo

1987 Wendy Ramshaw and David Watkins, Schmuckmuseum, Pforzheim

1987 *The New Spirit in Craft and Design*, Crafts Council Gallery, London

1988 *London-Amsterdam*, Crafts Council Gallery, London

1988 Johanna Hess-Dahm, Galerie Ra, Amsterdam

1988 *Biennale Svizzera Del Gioiello D'Arte Contemporaneo*, Villa Malpensata, Lugano

1988 *Hermann Jünger: Jewelry since 1945*, Schmuckmuseum, Pforzheim

1988 *Contemporary British Crafts*, Museum of Modern Art, Kyoto

1989 *British Jewelry*, Crafts Council Gallery, London

1989 *Function*, Rezac Gallery, Chicago

1989 *Constructions in Jewelry and Metal Objects*, Oriel Gallery, Cardiff

1989 Gijs Bakker Retrospective, Central Museum, Utrecht

1989 *Perth International Crafts Triennial*, Art Gallery of Western Australia

1989 *Ornamenta 1*, Schmuckmuseum, Pforzheim

1989 Anton Cepka and Vratislav Novak, Schmuckmuseum, Pforzheim

1990 *Body Art*, Security Pacific Gallery, Costa Mesa, California

1990 Caroline Broadhead Retrospective, Crafts Council Gallery, London

1991 Kevin Coates, Worshipful Company of Goldsmiths, London

1991 *Andrew Logan's An Artistic Adventure*, Museum of Modern Art, Oxford

1991 *Nel Linssen – Paper jewelry 1986–91*, Galerie Ra, Amsterdam

1991 *The Banqueting Table, 15 Years*, Galerie Ra, Amsterdam

1991 *Aggression in Jewelry*, Forum für Schmuck und Design, Cologne

1991 *The 20th Anniversary Show*, Electrum Gallery, London

1991 *Otto Künzli*, Stedelijk Museum, Amsterdam

1991 *Beauty is a Story*, Museum Het Kruithuis, 's-Hertogenbosch

1991 Friedrich Knupper (1947–87), Germanisches Nationalmuseum, Nuremberg

1992 *British Goldsmiths Today*, Worshipful Company of Goldsmiths, London

1992 *Neoteric Jewelry*, Snug Harbor Cultural Centre, Staten Island

1992 Brian Asquith/Elizabeth Gage/George Daniels, Worshipful Company of Goldsmiths, London

1992 Tone Vigeland, Kunstindustrimuseet, Oslo

1992 Beppe Kessler, Galerie Ra, Amsterdam

1993 *Schmuck Burg Giebichenstein 1970–1992*, Museum des Kunsthandwerks, Grassimuseum, Leipzig

1993 Emmy van Leersum (1930–84), Museum Het Kruithuis, 's-Hertogenbosch

1993 *13 Goldsmiths*, Bayerische Akademie der Schönen Künste, Munich

1993 *Kunststoff Schmuck Kunst 1923–1993*, Galerie Biro Munich

1993 *Facet 1*, Jewelry Biennale, Kunsthal, Rotterdam

1993 Giampaolo Babetto, Galleria Mauro, Milan

1993 *Gerd Rothmann Schmuck-Mabenahmen*, Deutsches Goldschmiedehaus, Hanau

1993 Manfred Bischoff Museum Het Kruithuis, 's-Hertogenbosch

1993 *The Chemistry Set – Patinated Metals*, Crafts Council Gallery, London

1993 *Ebbe Weiss-Weingart – Jewelry 1946–1993*, Schmuckmuseum Pforzheim

1993 *International Jewelry*, Design Forum, Helsinki

1993 Renate Heintze, Burg Giebichenstein Hochschule für Kunst und Design, Halle

1993 Carlier Makigawa, Helen Drutt Gallery, Philadelphia

1993 Marion Herbst Retrospective: 1968–93, Stedelijk Museum, Amsterdam

1994 *What is Jewelry?*, Crafts Council Gallery, London

PUBLICATIONS

Magazines

Each of these magazines gives some coverage to modern jewelry and each has been chosen for the high standard of both its editorial and illustrative content.

American Craft, 401 Park Avenue South, New York, NY 10016, USA

Art Aurea, Ebner Verlag, Karlstrasse 41, Postfach 3066, 7900 Ulm/Donau, Germany

Art Review, 20 Prescott Place, London SW4 6BT

Bÿvoorbeeld, Keizersgracht 135, 1015 CK Amsterdam, Holland

Craft Australia, 100 George Street, The Rocks, Sydney, NSW 2000, Australia

Crafts, Crafts Council, 44a Pentonville Road, Islington, London N1 9BY

Form & Function, Finnish Society of Craft and Design, Kurkeavuorenkatu 19a, 4b, 00130, Helsinki

Gold und Silber und Schmuck, Konradin-Verlag, D 7022 Leinfelden bei Stuttgart, Germany

Goldschmiede Zeitung, Rühle-Diebener-Verlag, Postfach 450, 7000 Stuttgart 70, Germany

Items, POB 3282, 2601 DG Delft, Holland

Jewelry Journal, 3–44–7 Honeo, Bunkyo Ku, Tokyo, Japan

Kunst & Handwerk, Postfach 8120, D 4000 Düsseldorf 1, Germany

Metalsmith, 2849 St Ann Drive, Green Bay, W1 54301, USA

Ornament, POB 35029, Los Angeles, CA 90035–0029, USA

Outline, Stichting Cosa, Oude Delft 1836, Delft, Holland

Books

There are many, many books devoted to do-it-yourself jewelry and very few devoted to giving any form of critical assessment of new jewelry. We offer two professional books on methods and technique, especially recommending Oppi Untracht's for its detailed, all-embracing character. The rest should interest those who find this book interesting.

Cartlidge, Barbara, *20th-Century Jewelry* (Abrams, New York, 1985)

Fisch, Arline, *Textile Techniques in Metal* (Van Nostrand Reinhold, New York, 1975)

Hinks, Peter, *Twentieth-century British Jewelry 1900–1980* (Faber & Faber, London, 1983; Faber & Faber Inc, Winchester Mass., 1983)

Hughes, Graham, *Modern Jewelry* (Studio Vista, London, 1963; Crown, New York, 1963)

Hughes, Graham, *The Art of Jewelry* (Studio Vista, London, 1972)

Reiling, Reinhold, *Goldschmiedekunst* (Verlag Ernst Wasmuth, Tübingen, 1978)

Schollmayer, Karl, *Neuer Schmuck* (Verlag Ernst Wasmuth, Tübingen, 1974)

Turner, Ralph, *Contemporary Jewelry: A Critical Assessment 1945–1975* (Studio Vista, London, 1976; Van Nostrand Reinhold, New York, 1976)

Untracht, Oppi, *Jewelry Concepts and Technology* (Doubleday, New York, 1982; Robert Hale, London, 1982)

Valcke, Johan, *Hedendaagse Juwelen in Belgie* (Mardaga, Liege, 1992)

Ward, Anne, and others, *The Ring: From Antiquity to the Twentieth Century* (Thames and Hudson, London, 1981)

Watkins, David, *The Best of Contemporary Jewelry* (Batsford, London, 1994)

Wilcox, David, *Body Jewelry* (Henry Regnery, Chicago, 1973; Pitman, London, 1973)

INDEX